Sexual Harassment in the Workplace

Mary L. Boland
Attorney at Law

First Edition: 2005

Published by: **Sphinx® Publishing, An Imprint of Sourcebooks, Inc.®**

<u>Naperville Office</u>
P.O. Box 4410
Naperville, Illinois 60567-4410
630-961-3900
Fax: 630-961-2168
www.sourcebooks.com
www.SphinxLegal.com

This publication is designed to provide accurate and authoritative information in regard
to the subject matter covered. It is sold with the understanding that the publisher is not
engaged in rendering legal, accounting, or other professional service. If legal advice or
other expert assistance is required, the services of a competent professional person
should be sought.
    From a Declaration of Principles Jointly Adopted by a Committee of the
    American Bar Association and a Committee of Publishers and Associations

This product is not a substitute for legal advice.
        Disclaimer required by Texas statutes.

Library of Congress Cataloging-in-Publication Data
Boland, Mary L.
   Sexual harassment in the workplace / by Mary L. Boland.-- 1st ed.
      p. cm.
   Includes bibliographical references and index.
   ISBN-13: 978-1-57248-527-3 (pbk. : alk. paper)
   ISBN-10: 1-57248-527-2 (pbk. : alk. paper)
   1. Sexual harassment--Law and legislation--United States. I. Title.

KF3467.B65 2005
344.7301'133--dc22

                                                                    2005027970

Printed and bound in the United States of America.
        BG — 10 9 8 7 6 5 4 3 2 1

Contents

SECTION ONE: OVERVIEW
OF SEXUAL HARASSMENT

SECTION THREE: REMEDIES

Fee Arrangements
Working with the Lawyer

Preface

Equal treatment at work is a civil right under federal and state laws. Sexual harassment is a type of sex discrimination involving unwelcome sexual conduct or pressure in the workplace. The laws say that no one should have to work in a *locker-room* atmosphere, and no one has the right to sexually bully another person at work. The laws apply to either sex, as both men and women can be harassers or harassed. However, sexual harassment is overwhelmingly a form of discrimination practiced by men against women. For this reason, many examples in this book will refer to the harasser as a man and the victim as a woman.

SEXUAL HARASSMENT OCCURS OFTEN

Sexual harassment is an immense problem in the workplace. Every year, tens of thousands of females and several thousand males come forward to report their experiences to their employers and federal and state agencies. A few file lawsuits to recover their losses.

In the 1970s, researchers estimated that as many as one out of every two women would become a victim of sexual harassment in her work environment. However, in the first survey of sexual harassment in the workplace, the numbers proved much higher. When *Redbook* magazine asked readers whether they had experienced sexual harassment, about 9,000 women responded. Nearly nine out of ten of the women reported that they had been targets of sexual harassment in their workplaces.[1]

Other surveys taken around that time produced equally high percentages, showing that 50–70% of women had been sexually harassed at work. For example, the *Redbook* article reports that in a random survey conducted by a naval officer, who used the same questionnaire to poll women on his base and in a nearby town in California, 81% of the women said they had experienced sexual harassment. A Cornell University survey also found that 70% of the respondents had experienced sexual harassment.

A 1992 survey in *Working Woman* magazine of over 9,000 readers showed that more than 60% of the women reported being harassed, and more than a third knew a coworker who had been harassed.[2]

The federal government has also documented a high rate of sexual harassment in the federal workforce. The *U.S. Merit Systems Protection Board* conducted a series of studies of sexual harassment in the federal government workforce in 1981, 1987, and 1994.[3] These surveys sampled thousands of federal workers, and showed that 42–44% of women reported being sexually harassed on the job.

The number of workers who complain of sexual harassment in the private and public workforces remains high. Employment discrimination complaints have tripled during the past decade. In fact, sexual harassment is now the basis for a third of all harassment claims handled by the federal agency charged with investigating sexual harassment in the workplace.

THE COST OF SEXUAL HARASSMENT

Sexual harassment is very costly. Lost career opportunities are difficult to measure, but statistics can tell part of the story. By the end of the 1980s, more than 90% of large companies reported cases and 40% of large companies had been sued for sexual harassment.[4] During a two-year period in the mid-1990s, sexual harassment cost the federal government (and taxpayers) more than $300 million. The Department of Labor estimates that private businesses lose around $1 billion annually due to sexual harassment. This figure does not include the millions of dollars of judgment awards in sexual harassment cases every year. (Over $150 million was awarded to victims in sexual harassment lawsuits in 1999.)

Introduction

Until recently, the law treated sexual harassment as a *personal problem* in the workplace. However, sexual harassment is a very serious form of employment discrimination, suffered mostly by women. Even after laws prohibiting harassment were in place, there was no real enforcement until the 1970s, when early surveys began to reveal the widespread nature of sexual harassment in the workplace. Anita Hill's testimony before Congress in 1991 opened the doors of justice to the tens of thousands of women and several thousand men who later came forward to complain of sexual harassment in their workplaces.

Even with increased sensitivity, complaints of sexual harassment in workplaces have continued to climb unacceptably over the last decade, more than tripling (according to federal statistics). Today, we know that sexual harassment costs hundreds of millions of dollars in job opportunities. The Department of Labor estimates that private businesses lose around $1 billion annually due to sexual harassment, and millions more in judgment awards in sexual harassment cases are entered every year. A zero-tolerance policy for sexual harassment is truly needed.

The goal of this book is to make you aware of your right to be free of sexual harassment at work. You will gain some practical preventive and responsive strategies to deal with sexually harassing situations. You will also specifically learn how to make a complaint of sexual harassment and understand how it is investigated by federal and state agencies. This book provides you with the resources to help you get the harassment to stop by working with your employer, or when necessary, filing a civil lawsuit to recover your losses.

Frequently Asked Questions about Sexual Harassment

What is sexual harassment?

Sexual harassment is a type of sexual discrimination in the workplace. It includes unwelcome sexual advances, requests for sexual favors, and sexual conduct that is directed toward a person because of gender.

Is there more than one kind of sexual harassment?

Yes. There are two recognized types of sexual harassment. One type is called *quid pro quo*, and includes a situation in which employment benefits are conditioned upon sexual favors. The second type is called a *hostile work environment*, in which the severe or pervasive conduct causes a hostile, intimidating, or offensive work environment. Many times, both types exist in the same case.

Could one incident constitute sexual harassment?

If sufficiently severe, like a demand for sex in return for keeping a job, one incident could constitute sexual harassment. Usually, though, when harassment is based on a hostile work environment, it requires a pattern of conduct.

Do I have to quit or be fired to file a complaint of sexual harassment?

No. An employer may still be held liable if you experience a negative change in work assignments, pay, or conditions.

What if my harasser is a coworker?

Your employer may still be liable for sexual harassment if the employer knew or should have known about it, but failed to take appropriate action.

If my harasser is of the same sex, is it still considered sexual harassment?

Yes. The law applies to same-sex and opposite-sex harassment equally.

Do I have to complain to my employer if I am sexually harassed?

In most cases, this is important to do, but there are cases in which the complaint can be filed without going through your employer's complaint process.

What is the best way to prevent sexual harassment?

An employer should have a policy and make it clear to employees that sexual harassment will not be tolerated. If sexual harassment occurs, the employer should take prompt steps to end the harassment.

What can I do if I think I am being harassed?

There are several strategies to consider in responding to sexual harassment. The simplest is a direct response, which is usually the most effective way to confront harassment. However, other choices may be important to consider, such as putting your concerns into a letter to your employer or contacting the local or federal EEOC office.

If I just ignore it, will it go away?

Not likely. Harassers do not usually stop on their own. The best way to show that the conduct is unwelcome is to take some action to have it stopped.

Does every employer need a sexual harassment policy?

Yes. While federal law extends to employers of fifteen or more, many states have laws that apply to smaller employers and require these employers to have anti-harassment policies.

Section One:
Overview of Sexual Harassment

chapter one:
Dynamics
of Sexual Harassment

Sexual harassment laws were designed to prevent employers from permitting this form of discrimination in the workplace. Supervisors, coworkers, and even nonemployees (under certain circumstances) can commit sexual harassment. *Supervisors* include employees with sufficient authority or power that their acts are considered those of the employer. Supervisors can have direct authority over an employee or can make certain decisions about that employee. For instance, a supervisor who is responsible for making out the daily work log would qualify just as much as the one who has the power to promote employees.

Supervisors can engage in more forms of sexual harassment because of the authority given, so their acts are considered the acts of the company or employer. In these cases, it is easier to hold the company responsible. Because nonemployees and most coworkers do not have authority to make supervisory decisions, the rules to determine their responsibility for sexual harassment are somewhat different. Most often, the complaint is that the sexual harassment has caused a hostile work environment. In a suit involving coworkers and nonemployees, the employer must show that it exercised due care to prevent harassment, and corrected the problem when it became aware of the harassment. These rules give companies a strong incentive to take care to prevent sexual harassment. Employees are also encouraged to report harassment promptly when possible. Employees who are sexually harassed are also protected from retaliation for complaining about it.

WHY SEXUAL HARASSMENT OCCURS

Sexual harassment is more about exercising power than about sex. The abuse of power is the key to understanding why sexual harassment occurs.

Harassment Begins Early

Sexually harassing conduct begins long before the workplace. In fact, girls in the third grade have reported being targeted for sexual harassment, and sexually harassing conduct increasingly becomes more common as students move through elementary and high school. In one comprehensive study of more than 1,600 students, those who admitted that they had harassed other students explained that, "it's just a part of school life. A lot of people do it. It's no big deal."[5] Researchers believe that the true reasons—to assert power and induce fear in their victims—lay the real foundation for sexual harassment. The power and intimidation of harassment continues and develops throughout high school, in the hazing behaviors of college, and finally comes out in the workplace.

Sexual Harassment Knows No Job Descriptions

It might be surprising to realize that sexual harassment occurs in all types of workplaces. In fact, in the first sexual harassment survey of 9,000 women, there was little difference in the type of workplace identified by women who said they were sexually harassed.

Professional and nonprofessional women are targeted for harassment, and it happens in the public and private sectors. As one writer noted, "The female workers of Wall Street and Wal-Mart would appear worlds apart. Their shared experience became apparent...as securities giant Morgan Stanley agreed to pay $54 million to settle a sex-discrimination case. That move came less than a month after a judge ruled a lawsuit against Wal-Mart can proceed as a class action covering about 1.6 million women. The claims in each case are strikingly similar."[6]

Sexual Stereotyping

One factor that is present in a high percentage of sexual harassment cases is a workplace that encourages *traditional* attitudes towards women.

These workplaces have attitudes that include the following.
- She does not belong in this job.
- She does not belong in the workplace.
- She is taking the place of a man who needs the job.
- She is being paid more than a woman ought to earn.
- She is just at this job to find a husband.

Stereotypical views of women pose serious risks for women in a workplace. One expert explained that, "when sex comes into the workplace, women are profoundly affected in their job performance and in their ability to do their jobs without being bothered by it." This is because men and women perceive the existence of sexual harassment differently. Fear of harassment for women may also involve the very real potential risk of harm, if obnoxious words or jokes turn into threats or sexual violence. Therefore, women who are sexually harassed are more likely to be negatively affected by it than are males.

Male-Dominated Workplaces

High levels of sexual harassment exist when there is a low number of women in the workplace. In fact, the women in jobs that are nontraditional for women are more likely to be sexually harassed. Indeed, high numbers of female doctors and investment bankers have reported sexual harassment.[7]

When women do break into these fields and are successful, men may feel threatened by the entry of females. Sexual harassment is one way to *put down* a woman, to *keep her in her place*, and to increase the feeling of power by the harasser. If the woman becomes frustrated enough, she may begin to make mistakes, get sick, be absent from work, or fail to carry out the job, leaving the harasser with the satisfaction of knowing that *women just cannot make it in a man's world*.

When few female workers are present in a workplace, they are singled out for scrutiny and are the focus of attention for the rumor mill. When these workers make a mistake on the job, it typically causes extreme responses from the men who comprise the majority group. Mistakes that would be minor if a male worker committed them become perceived as much worse when one of the few female workers commits them.

In a survey of female coal miners, 17% reported having been physically attacked on the job, 53% reported propositions from their supervisors on at least one occasion, and 76% reported propositions from a coworker.[8] A study of women employed in the male-populated occupations of engineering and management also reported a high percentage of sexual harassment.[9] The similarity between the coal miners and the engineers and managers was that these women occupied traditionally male jobs.

Sexual Harassment in Policing

One occupation in which sexual harassment is all too often found is policing. In 2001, women comprised only 12.7% of all police officers nationwide—only about 4% more than in 1990, when women made up 9% of officers.[10] Women held about 7% of sworn top command law enforcement positions in large agencies, but only 4% in smaller or rural agencies, and just 9% of supervisory positions in these departments. More than 56% of the agencies surveyed reported no women in top command positions.

Given the low numbers of women in policing, it should come as no surprise that numerous cases of sexual harassment are reported every year in police agencies throughout the country. For example, in 1995, the Los Angeles Police Department settled a sexual harassment case involving a 1990 rape of a female officer. The female officer was sexually assaulted by a male officer who followed her into the bathroom when she was ill from intoxication. At the time of the settlement, there were over two dozen sexual harassment cases pending filed by female officers in the department. Prior to settling the case, the victim testified to repeated incidents of harassment by male officers while she was on duty, starting when she joined the department in 1987 until she left patrol in 1992.[11]

Similarly, in Grand Rapids, Michigan, nine female police officers sued the city and its police department, naming more than twenty male officers and implicating several command-level officers in allegations of sexual harassment occurring between 1996 and 2000. Allegations included:

- unwanted physical advances;
- crude and demeaning insults;
- assignments to do *women's work*, such as filing;
- death threats from male officers while on the job;
- a male sergeant pointed a loaded gun at one of the female officers and warned her to keep quiet about on-duty sexual advances; and,
- exclusions from promotions and assignments.

Besides the nine women who filed the lawsuit, nearly thirty current and past female officers and trainees are listed in the suit as possible victims. Of the city's nearly four hundred police officers, about fifty are women.[12]

For the same reasons, numerous cases of sexual harassment have occurred in fire departments. For example, until 1978, San Francisco policy prohibited women from becoming firefighters. It took almost ten years until the first female firefighter was hired in 1987. Today, only about 12% of firefighters nationwide are women. When these fields purposefully make it difficult for women to gain and keep employment, and to be fairly promoted, millions of taxpayer dollars devoted to training these officers and civilian workers is lost. Women who have complained about harassment have also been retaliated against. A former police officer who founded the National Center for Women & Policing said that, "it's really hard for those who complain. Very few women who have filed lawsuits are ever able to get a job in law enforcement. It's like they violated that old culture, that code of silence, and are labeled troublemakers."[13]

Unfortunately, in many cases, it has been left to the courts to enforce a change in these attitudes. In March of 1998, Nancy Suders was hired by the Pennsylvania State Police to work as a communications operator. Suders complained that in the barracks, officers—including several of her supervisors—engaged in a constant pattern of abuse using sexually explicit words, gestures, and conversations about sex with animals. When Suders tried to confront the officers, they increased the harassment and began to make negative comments about her job performance. Suders went to her Equal Employment Opportunity Officer, who told her to file a complaint, but did not help her find the right form to do so.

Suders had also taken a computer skills test several times. Each time, her supervisors told her she had failed. Suders suspected otherwise and she found her exams in a drawer in the women's locker room. The supervisors found out that the tests were missing and suspected Suders had taken them. They put theft detection powder on the drawer. When Suders attempted to return the exams, her hands turned blue. The officers then arrested her, put her in handcuffs, and questioned her as if she was a criminal suspect. Suders was finally allowed to leave when she agreed to resign. The United States Supreme Court decided that female police personnel do not have to accept these type of intolerable working conditions, and that any reasonable person in

Suders' position would have felt compelled to resign. (*Pennsylvania State Police v. Suders*, 542 U.S. 129 (2004).)

Sexual Harassment is Common in the Military

About half of the women in the Air Force, Army, and Navy reported sexual harassment. In the national surveys of federal workers conducted by the Merit Systems Protection Board in 1996, cases of rape in the Army surfaced. When the Army established a sexual harassment hotline, it received nearly 6,600 complaints in its first two months.

In one particularly outrageous example, a female helicopter pilot was one of more than eighty women who said drunken Navy and Marine pilots at the 1991 Tailhook convention sexually assaulted them.[14] When she stepped out of an elevator in her hotel, she was forced to run a gauntlet of officers who grabbed at her breasts, crotch, and buttocks, and attempted to tear her clothes from her body. When her complaints to her boss went nowhere, she filed a formal complaint with the Navy before resigning her commission. She eventually filed a civil lawsuit and won $5 million in damages.

The Navy went on to determine that 117 officers were "implicated in one or more incidents of indecent assault, indecent exposure, conduct unbecoming an officer, or failure to act in a proper leadership capacity." Eventually, over seventy officers—including admirals, captains, and commanders of the Navy and Marines—were disciplined. Because of this case, there were changes of policy within the U.S. military. Still, as of 1999, there were just three hundred women among the 10,000 pilots in the Navy and Marines.

Cases of sexual harassment in the military continue to be reported, like the December 1999 case of an Army drill sergeant who was court-martialed for fondling or sexually harassing twenty female recruits in his command. The drill sergeant had sexually harassed and assaulted female trainees from July 1995 until April 1996, when he was reported by a recruit who said he followed her into the female sleeping bay and rubbed his hand across her hair and breast. He then engaged in an effort to dissuade her from cooperating in the investigation and tried to get another female recruit to wrongfully offer a statement against her. (*U.S. v. Barner*, 00-0431 (U.S. Ct. of App., Armed Forces 2001).)

More recently, the Department of Defense developed new guidelines to combat sexual harassment after surveys of the military academies showed that one in seven female students had been sexually harassed or assaulted in the spring of 2004. Only about one-third of these incidents were ever formally reported. The new policy, implemented in June, 2005, encourages confidential reports to permit increased efforts to rid the military academies of sexual misconduct.

Sexualized Environment

Another factor that contributes to sex stereotyping is the climate of the workplace. For example, when profanities are common in the workplace, women are three times more likely to be treated as sex objects than where profanity is not tolerated. When sexual joking is common in a work environment, stereotyping of women as sex objects is three to seven times more likely to occur. These workplaces are also more dangerous for women. In one study, almost 50% of women working in nonprofessional capacities were subjected to physical acts as part of the sexual harassment.

A workplace that is full of sexist pictures, joking, or sexual slurs may contribute to the view of women as stereotypical sex objects. For example, welder Lois Robinson was one of only a handful of women who worked at Jacksonville Shipyards. Pornography was commonly displayed openly on the walls of the workplace. Even supervisors had pictures of nude women hanging on their walls. Robinson's coworkers constantly made sexual comments and advances directed at her and other female workers. The court found that there is a connection between the presence of pictures and sexual comments, and the level of sexual preoccupation of some male workers whose conduct has sexual overtones towards female workers. The court also found that these behaviors can constitute a hostile working environment. (*Robinson v. Jacksonville Shipyards, Inc.*, 760 F. Supp. 1486 (M.D. Fla. 1991).)

As one court has noted:

> *[T]he effect of pornography on workplace equality is obvious. Pornography on an employer's wall or desk communicates a message about the way he views women, a view strikingly at odds with the way women wish to be viewed in the workplace. Depending upon the material in question, it may communicate that women should be the objects of sexual aggression, that they are submissive slaves to male desires, or that their most salient and desirable attributes are sexual. Any of these images may communicate to male coworkers that it is acceptable to view women in a predominately sexual way. All of the views to some extent detract from the image most women*

in the workplace would like to project: that of the profes-
sional, credible coworker. (EEOC v. Dial Corp., 156 F.
Supp. 2d 926 (N.D. Ill. 2001).)

Whatever the job environment, workers have a right not to be sexually harassed. A federal jury made that clear to a Hooters restaurant when it awarded nearly $300,000 in damages to a former *Hooters girl*. Three other girls at the same restaurant settled their claims. These workers were subjected to peepholes in their dressing room and managers who asked the girls out on dates, slapped them on the buttocks, touched them inappropriately, and used offensive sexual language.[15]

Male Supervisors

As shown in the *Hooters* example, the type of power structure in a workplace also affects the level of sexual harassment. Commonly, workers affected by the sexualized working conditions are women, but the people who have the power to decide what to do about it are men. So men—who are typically the supervisors in this type of workplace and are the ones to get complaints from women—tend to ignore or minimize the complaints.

In workplaces where men control and few women work in a given location, if a woman complains about a man who exposed himself to her, it is the woman that will be perceived as the problem. She may become the subject of rumors, while the male worker will not likely be disciplined, or if disciplined, it will be slight. In one court case, this took the form of the supervisor who said that the woman's complaint that her coworker exposed himself to her was "one person's word against another's." The same thing may happen in a workplace that has sexualized pictures of women displayed. She may be seen in such a workplace as a *complainer* and a *problem* employee. Other workers may speculate on her sexuality or try to find out *what is wrong with her*.

Women who work in this type of workplace may begin to monitor their own behavior to try to avoid sexual attention from males in the workplace. They may try to join in the stereotyping, becoming overly *sexy* or *flirty*, telling dirty jokes so that they can *fit in* and avoid being ostracized. Some women may become rigid—refusing to engage in the workplace banter—and therefore become the focus of intensified harassment, as the next case shows.

A female plant worker reported that a male coworker made various sexual comments about her body. Nothing was done about her complaint, and the coworker continued his pattern of harassment, soon joined by another. The two were boldly making comments to others and discussing graffiti appearing on the men's bathroom walls. She continued to report these actions to no avail. Her own supervisor grabbed her breast and asked her out for drinks at a local bar. She declined, and complained to a higher-up, who said he would talk to the supervisor and not to take him too seriously.

Male coworkers developed sexualized nicknames for her, and her supervisor gave her a performance review form containing sexual content. Other supervisors joined in the sexualized commentary directed at this worker. Untrue rumors were constantly circulated about her sexual activities. Other coworkers began to target her for sexual conversations and gestures. She continued to complain and was terminated in a *workforce reduction*, even though the company approved a budget that forecasted an increase just three days before she was fired. Further, no other employee was terminated as a result of the *downsizing*. (*Baty v. Williamette Ind., Inc.*, 172 F.3d 1232 (10th Cir. 1999).)

Sexual Harassment and Prejudice

It is common for people to associate with others who are like themselves. Some call this the *like me syndrome*. As in life, work relationships and friendships are often formed with persons who look and act like us. But when these views impact the ability to be hired or promoted in the workplace, it is called *unlawful discrimination*.

Supervisors may make decisions out of a bias or prejudice that favors workers *like* them. For example, supervisors have the power to make choices, such as whether to hire a job applicant or who to promote. Those with a bias or prejudice may hire or promote persons who look and act like themselves. They may also rely on these biases to make decisions on who to send to training or who to give the more *high-profile* projects to. For example, this type of supervisor may believe *women are too weak to be in management*. Therefore, the supervisor may not select a female employee for a position in line with management opportunities, or may make more subtle choices, like failing to send her to necessary training so that she is not eligible for promotion. This *like me* prejudice may also be found in work evaluations. A worker who is perceived of as *different* may get tougher appraisals of their performance.

One of the most obvious forms of prejudice is paying less to women as compared to men for the same job. Today, women overall only earn about seventy-five cents for every dollar a man makes. Even when women are promoted, they earn only a relative sixty-nine cents for the same manager or executive who is a man. Only about 15% of women are at the very top levels in management. One recent study found that even though 60% of male workers had children at home, women workers who were mothers earned even less than women without children.

STOPPING SEXUAL HARASSMENT

Employers are charged with keeping their workplaces free of sexual harassment. The changes in the law have forced more employers to face claims, and therefore, to confront this serious and widespread problem. Early cases granted little relief to women who were entering traditionally male jobs. They were told to deal with the culture of the workplace, however raunchy that was. After all, a woman who wanted to work in such an environment would not think it harassing or she would not keep working there. But this attitude has changed, thanks to the many workers who refused to accept that to get or keep a job, women were required to be treated as sexual objects or harassed simply because they were women.

As you will learn in later chapters of this book, sexual harassment rarely stops by itself. You will usually need to take action, and soon. The most effective action is to be direct—say or write something—and do it immediately, before it escalates (as it so often does). Talk to a supportive friend or coworker, keep good records, and most of all, take care of yourself. Do not keep it a secret. If it is safe to do so, notify your employer.

As more women go public with their claims, employers are taking notice. A New York jury recently awarded a female salesperson for Europe's largest bank more than $29 million.

She worked in a hostile environment with a supervisor who demeaned her, and she was excluded from client meetings held at strip clubs. Perhaps as important as the award is the fact that the plaintiff refused to permit the employer to keep the settlement confidential.[16]

As seen in a later section of this book, more employers are responding to these large damage awards by developing anti-sexual harassment policies and taking immediate steps to correct harassing situations. Many have instituted training programs. In 2005, California became the first state to mandate sexual harassment training for all employers with fifty or more employees.

chapter two:
Laws

Laws that prohibit sexual harassment exist on the federal, state, and local level. The federal antidiscrimination law that prohibits sexual harassment in the workplace is *Title VII* of the *Civil Rights Act of 1964*. Most states have also passed Fair Employment Practice Acts that are modeled after federal laws. All states and some municipalities have passed antidiscrimination laws, and provide another option to pursue a claim of employment discrimination. The conduct underlying sexual harassment may form the basis of private lawsuits. In some cases, it may also be prohibited by criminal laws.

TITLE VII OF THE CIVIL RIGHTS ACT

The relevant part of Title VII of the Civil Rights Act can be found in Appendix B. If you read the law, you will realize that the words "sexual harassment" do not appear in the Civil Rights law at all. This is because making sex a category of discrimination was added shortly before the bill was to be voted on in Congress in an effort to stop the bill from passing. However, the bill passed anyway, making sex discrimination in the workplace illegal in 1964.

Title VII makes employment discrimination based on sex illegal, but allows for "bona fide occupational qualification" exceptions, which permit an employer to establish certain requirements that employees must meet to hold a job. It covers those who apply for a job as well as employees, but only applies to employers with fifteen or more workers. It also prohibits retaliation against any person who reports or assists in the investigation of sexual harassment. (For more information on federal law, see Appendix B.)

Even though Title VII of the Civil Rights Act became effective in 1964, it was not until more than a decade later that a few courts were even willing to recognize sexual harassment as a form of prohibited sex discrimination. Until the mid-1970s, courts viewed complaints of sexual harassment as *personal relationship* problems instead of discrimination. For example, in 1975, two women filed suit, stating that they were forced to resign from their jobs because their supervisor made repeated sexual advances towards them. The court said that it would be "ludicrous" to permit the women to proceed with a lawsuit because of their supervisor's *amorous* advances, and so dismissed the women's complaint.

But some courts began to recognize the legal claim of sexual harassment. For example, in 1976, a worker filed suit because her supervisor retaliated for her refusal to engage in sex with him by refusing to supervise her or to explain to her how to perform her job, and then reprimanding her when she did it wrong. The employer claimed she was fired for poor work performance, and that the conduct of its supervisor was "an isolated personal incident which should not be the concern of the courts." The court disagreed and said it was sex discrimination.

STATE FAIR EMPLOYMENT PRACTICE ACTS

All states have passed at least one law that covers discrimination in employment; and nearly all states have specific sexual harassment laws modeled after Title VII of the federal law. A few states, like Georgia and Mississippi, do not have specific laws that cover sexual harassment, so federal law will govern.

State laws differ considerably in their scope and coverage. Some states, like Arizona and Illinois, include employers if they have just one employee; others begin coverage of employers with just a few employees. These states permit claims against employers that would not be covered by the federal law, which begins coverage when an employer reaches fifteen employees. Many states use the federal limit of fifteen employees.

States also differ in the type and amount of damages permitted. Some states, which follow federal law, cap the amount recoverable for compensatory and punitive damages. Other states are even more restrictive. For example, Delaware, Louisiana, New Mexico, and Pennsylvania, unlike federal law, do not permit recovery of punitive damages. Kansas limits compensatory losses to a few thousand dollars. New York does not cap compensatory damages, but it does not allow for punitive damages. Other states, like California, Connecticut, Florida, Kentucky, and New Jersey, do not impose limits on the amount of damages recoverable and so are more favorable than federal law. Other states, like Colorado, Idaho, and Virginia, limit recovery of attorney's fees.

Some states cover more types of workers than federal law. For example, unlike many states, in California and Massachusetts, nonsupervisory coworkers can be held personally liable for

sexual harassment. In Massachusetts, any worker who partici-
pates in the sexual harassment can be held liable.

A complaint of sexual harassment under Title VII or the state
fair employment law may be filed with the appropriate local,
state, or federal agency charged with investigating sexual
harassment. On the federal level, the *Equal Employment
Opportunity Commission* (EEOC) is charged with investigating
complaints of sexual harassment. Most states have separate
fair employment practice agencies (sometimes called FEPAs).
Generally, agencies follow their own rules for investigating
complaints. (To find your state's law, filing procedures, and
agency, see Appendix C.)

LOCAL MUNICIPAL CODES

Many cities and municipalities have adopted ordinances and resolutions on sexual harassment in the workplace. These codes
set forth guidelines for handling violations of the policy and to
specify the related complaint-handling procedure. For example,
the Cook County, *Illinois Human Rights Ordinance* applies to
Cook County employers with one or more employees, and
specifically prohibits sexual harassment. These ordinances may
be broader than state or federal laws.

These ordinances may hold an employer strictly responsible for
the conduct of its supervisors. They also may hold the employer
responsible for acts of sexual harassment between coworkers in
the workplace where the employer (or its agents or supervisory
employees) knew or should have known of the conduct, unless
it can show that it took immediate and appropriate corrective
action. Finally, the ordinances may also extend to hold an

employer responsible for the acts of nonemployees for sexual harassment of employees in the workplace. Some municipalities also permit complaints to be filed and investigated locally. To learn whether your jurisdiction has a local code prohibiting sexual harassment, check with the state fair employment practice agency. (see Appendix C.)

PRIVATE TORT CLAIMS

Sexual harassment may also be the subject of a private civil case. The types of claims vary and are covered by state laws addressing private lawsuits, such as assault and battery, false imprisonment, libel, slander, breach of contract, and other claims. In many cases, more than one claim will be present. Each of these claims requires a different kind of proof. The victim of harassment files the claims directly with a court in a lawsuit and is responsible to investigate private claims that form the basis for tort lawsuits.

CRIMINAL LAWS

More severe forms of sexual harassment may also be crimes under local or state laws. These may include sexual abuse, sexual assault, rape, and other forms of physical assault. The victim can file minor crimes complaints directly with the police or a court, but prosecutors must file more severe claims. Law enforcement investigates criminal offenses.

chapter three:
Types of Sexual Harassment

When employment is conditioned on submission to sexual advances, or when unwelcomed sexual conduct is so severe and pervasive that a reasonable employee would find it to be an offensive working environment, then it constitutes sexual harassment. Courts have carved out different standards for sexual harassment, depending on the conduct and who is doing the harassing. Ultimately, each case turns on its own facts—how severe the conduct was, who did it, and how the conduct impacted the victim of the harassment.

HARASSING CONDUCT: A CONTINUUM OF HARM

Sexually harassing behavior involves a range of conduct, from minor offensive words or acts to forced sexual activity and even rape. While there is no minimum level for harassing conduct under the law, the general rule is that the more severe the conduct, the less number of times it has to occur. For example, a single sexual advance may be enough to show sexual harassment if it is connected to granting or denying employment benefits.

However, unless the conduct is very serious, a single incident of offensive sexual conduct or comment generally does not create a hostile environment. This type of claim usually requires a showing of a pattern offensive conduct. A single, unusually severe incident of harassment may be sufficient, however. For example, a single incident of touching a coworker's intimate body areas is considered severe sexual harassment.

As you read the following section explaining the conduct that has been identified in sexual harassment claims, keep in mind that not all of this type of conduct will be considered severe enough to form the basis for a legal claim of sexual harassment. Most often, there are several types of sexually harassing behaviors present in the same case.

The less physically threatening forms of sexually harassing behaviors are also the most commonly reported. These include the following forms of harassment.

- *Sexual Joking*. Sexual harassment exists where the conduct is *unwelcome*. Therefore, while some women think that if they join in the joking it will lessen the impact of the harassment, it may, in fact, work against them. It provides evidence that they did not find it objectionable or offensive, and may result in a determination that they were not victims of a hostile environment. In fact, going along with the jokes is not effective in stopping harassment, and in a significant number of cases, just makes it worse.

As unfair as it may seem, the law permits review of *provocative dress*, *bad language*, and other conduct of the target of harassment. There are several cases in which complaints of sexual harassment were denied because the targets *participated in sexual horseplay* or used vulgar or foul language themselves. Ultimately, the determination of whether a work environment is hostile is made after reviewing all of the circumstances and the context in which the behavior occurred.

- *Sexist Words.* Sometimes sexual harassment takes the form of words that are directed at females in general, including:
  - calling a woman "doll," "babe," "sweetie," or "honey";
  - using sexist phrases, like "dumb blondes";
  - claiming that "women cry more" or are "too emotional";
  - asking male workers to "think above their belt buckles";
  - announcing that "women can't manage" or "workers will not work for a woman";
  - stating that "some jobs are just women's work"; or,
  - suggesting that women should be "barefoot and pregnant."

- *Sexist Behavior.* A harasser's physical conduct may also contribute to a sexually harassing environment. Examples of sexually harassing conduct without words include:
  - looking up and down a person's body;
  - staring at someone;
  - cornering a person or blocking a person's path;
  - following the person;
  - giving personal gifts;
  - hanging around a person;
  - intentionally standing too close to or brushing against a person;

- looking up a skirt or down a blouse;
- pulling a person onto one's lap;
- displaying sexist or sexual calendars;
- writing sexist or sexual graffiti;
- massaging or touching a person's clothing, hair, or body;
- hugging, kissing, patting, or stroking;
- touching or rubbing oneself sexually around another person;
- making facial expressions such as winking, throwing kisses, or licking lips;
- making sexual gestures with hands or through body movements; or,
- making catcalls, whistling suggestively, or engaging in lip smacking.
- *Sexual Advances.* Some harassment may include physical and verbal sexual advances towards one or more victims. Examples of these include:
  - turning discussions to sexual topics;
  - telling sexually explicit or suggestive jokes or stories;
  - asking about sexual fantasies, experiences, preferences, or history;
  - making sexual comments or innuendos;
  - telling lies or spreading rumors about a person's sex life;
  - asking personal questions about social or sexual life;
  - making sexual comments about a person's clothing, anatomy, or looks;
  - repeatedly asking out a person who is not interested; or,
  - making harassing phone calls or emails.

Requests for Sex

This type of sexually harassing behavior typically occurs when a supervisor suggests or promises benefits, like a promotion or wage increase, if the victim engages in sexual activity. These requests include:

- asking a person to *spend the night*;
- asking a person to have an affair; or,
- asking a person to have sex or to engage in sexual conduct.

Sexual Intimidation

This type of coercion occurs when there is a warning that the employee will lose his or her job or lose a job benefit unless the he or she agrees to engage in a sexual activity. For example, telling a person to go to a motel to *negotiate* a raise or ordering a person to provide sexual services to avoid a transfer.

Sexual Criminal Conduct

Less common, but more violent, sexually harassing conduct may include:

- threats of harm;
- forced sexual touching; or,
- attempted or completed sexual assault.

Any attempted or completed grabbing, touching, or forcing sexual activity without consent is a sexual crime.

CATEGORIES OF SEXUAL HARASSMENT

Sexual harassment claims fall into two broad categories: *quid pro quo* (*something for something*) and *hostile environment*. Both types of claims can exist in the same case.

Quid Pro Quo

Quid pro quo sexual harassment usually involves a supervisor who has the power to make decisions about the employee, based on whether he or she submits to sexual demands.

The two legally required elements of a quid pro quo case are:

1. an employee is subject to unwelcome sexual advances and
2. submission to the sexual advances is a condition of a job benefit or refusal to submit resulted in a detriment.

Quid pro quo cases were the first type of sexual harassment to be recognized by the Supreme Court. In 1986, in the case of *Meritor Savings Bank v. Vinson*, 477 U.S. 57, a female bank employee was sexually harassed both inside and outside of work by her supervisor, who was the vice president of the bank. She had worked at the bank for four years before she took a sick leave and was fired for failing to return to work. She filed suit and explained that she began as a teller and, based on her work performance, was promoted to assistant branch manager. During her probationary period as a trainee teller, the supervisor had treated her much like a daughter. He made no sexual advances during that time.

Later, he invited her out to dinner. At dinner, he suggested that they go to a motel and have sex. At first she refused, but out of fear of losing her job she agreed. After that, at her supervisor's repeated demands, she had sex at least forty times over a four-year period, usually at the bank, both during and after business hours. He also fondled her in front of other employees, followed her into the women's rest room, exposed himself to her, and raped her on several occasions. There was also evidence that the supervisor had inappropriately touched other female bank employees. Because she was afraid of him, the victim never reported this harassment to the bank.

Like many other courts during that time, the trial judge in the *Meritor* case found that she voluntarily had a relationship with her supervisor and it had nothing to do with her employment at the bank. She appealed to the federal appellate court, and it disagreed with the trial court, stating that her supervisor's demands for sex were a condition of employment and were not welcomed by her.

This time, the employer appealed, and the case went to the Supreme Court of the United States. There, the Supreme Court held that the sexual conduct was clearly not welcomed by her since she was required to submit to sex or face being fired if she refused. The Court said that it was "demeaning and disconcerting" for a worker to have to "run a gauntlet of sexual abuse in return for the privilege of being allowed to work and make a living." With these words, courts opened their doors to the quid pro quo form of sexual harassment.

Today, many of the issues have been answered in quid pro quo cases. Cases have determined that an applicant for a job is included as a person who is protected by the law. It is quid pro quo sexual harassment if a job applicant refuses the sexual demands of an employee who makes hiring decisions (or tells her that he does) and is denied the job. It may also be quid pro quo sexual harassment if an applicant for a job is rejected in favor of another, less qualified person, simply because the person hired submitted to the sexual demands of the supervisor.

Many cases have determined what a *sexual advance* is. Making sexual activity a condition of the job is now clearly understood as quid pro quo sexual harassment. Also, demonstrating that the victim was hired, fired, demoted, or otherwise actually affected is also fairly easy to show. However, a few issues continue to be raised in this type of sexual harassment case, such as former intimate relationships or in situations of favoritism.

Hostile Environment

The second type of sexual harassment, *hostile environment*, was first recognized in 1980 with the adoption of the Equal Employment Opportunity Commission's guidelines on sexual harassment. A hostile work environment case is established when the environment becomes so intimidating or offensive that it changes the conditions of the job. Unlike the usual quid pro quo case, a hostile environment can be caused by the sexual harassment of coworkers, third parties, and supervisors.

As one court put it: "A work environment consumed by remarks that intimidate, ridicule, and maliciously demean the status of women can create an environment that is as hostile as an environment that contains unwanted sexual advances." (*Smith v. First Union National Bank*, 202 F.3d 234, 242 (4th Cir. 2000).)

Elements

Hostile environment cases are not as easy to identify as quid pro quo cases, because there is no exact formula that determines what constitutes a hostile environment. The victim may not be able to show a job loss or pay cut, but instead must show that the work environment is so hostile that it affects his or her working conditions. The legal elements of a hostile environment case are:

- an employee was subject to unwelcome sexual harassment; and,
- the harassment unreasonably interfered with the employee's work performance; or,
- the harassment created an intimidating, hostile, or offensive environment.

Whether an environment is hostile is determined by examining how many times the conduct occurred, the severity of the conduct, and the effect it had on the victim. All of the circumstances of the environment are examined, including:

- the conduct itself (nature, type, how often, for how long, and where the conduct occurred);
- the persons involved (age and sex of the parties, and the number of accused);
- whether an accused harasser was in a position of power;
- whether the conduct negatively affected the work environment; and,
- whether any other incidents of sexual harassment occurred in the workplace.

It is important to note that the conduct will always be viewed in the context of the environment it occurs in. For example, a coach slapping a football player on the buttocks in congratulations for a play will not be sexual harassment, where it is considered the norm or a part of the roughhousing of the game. But, if back in the office, the same coach slaps the buttocks of the secretary, a reasonable person could consider that behavior abusive.

Sufficiently Severe or Pervasive

In considering whether sexual harassment is *sufficiently severe or pervasive* to alter the conditions of an employee's work and create an abusive environment, courts look at all of the circumstances presented through the eyes of a reasonable person, including:

- how often the harassing conduct occurred;
- how severe the conduct was;
- whether the conduct was physically threatening or humiliating;
- whether the conduct unreasonably interfered with the victim's work performance; and,
- the presence of psychological harm to the victim.

The line is not always clear on what conduct is severe enough or pervasive enough to constitute a legal claim of sexual harassment. Each claim is considered based on its own circumstances.

ISSUES IN SEXUAL HARASSMENT

More recent cases have blurred the line between the two types of sexual harassment, and most cases present a combination of these types of claims. The following issues continue to arise in sexual harassment cases.

Conduct Must Be Unwelcome

Romantic relationships may be present in the workplace setting. Sexual harassment laws do not change this. Courts have said that the antidiscrimination laws are not designed to create a *code of conduct* in a workplace.

At one end of the continuum of conduct, sexual threats or forced violence will be presumed to be unwelcome. It also seems to be common sense that if a person objects to sexual comments, jokes, behavior, advances, and so on, then that person believes the conduct is unwelcome. However, in the absence of threats or violence, the law requires that there be some proof that the conduct is unwelcome.

Courts have made it clear, though, that *unwelcome* is not the same thing as *voluntary* behavior. For example, engaging in sex to keep a job may be a voluntary act, but certainly one that is not welcomed by the victim of harassment.

Isolated Comments

Because the sexual harassment has to literally *change the conditions* of the environment, the United States Supreme Court has said that a single sexual comment or remark, even if it was obnoxious or demeaning, is not enough, by itself, to demonstrate a hostile environment. This is also why an instance of flirting, innuendo, and even isolated obscenity or vulgarity will not establish the existence of a hostile environment. However, it is also true that there is no clear minimum level of conduct that must be shown. For example, if a single derogatory comment is repeated by many different workers, the conduct is no longer isolated and can be considered sexually harassing. It is also true that the more severe the harassment, the less need there is to show that it has been repeated.

Former Relationship

Proving that the conduct was unwelcome becomes a special point of contention in cases where there was a former intimate relationship between the parties. For example, in one case, a supervisor convinced his female employee to have sex with him. After she broke it off, he agreed to treat her in a professional manner, but when she asked about a promotion, the supervisor told her he was still sexually attracted to her and suggested that they have sex. She refused and got the promotion anyway, but he later told her that she owed him for her promotion. (*Henningsen v. Worldcom*, 9 P.3d 948 (Wash.App. 2000).)

Because the conduct was once welcomed, the person who has ended the relationship must make it clear to the other person that further sexual advances are no longer welcome. Courts look to see how the person who complains of sexual harassment put the former spouse or significant other on notice that the relationship had ended and that the advances were no longer welcome. The victim should tell the manager, coworkers, and other appropriate persons that the relationship is over. Also, the victim must tell the harasser that the conduct is no longer welcome. This can be done in person, but sending a letter or other written document stating that further advances are not welcome may be helpful to show a present intent that the conduct is not—and will not be—welcome.

Favoritism

Favoritism arises when a supervisor promotes his girlfriend to a position you were also qualified for. If the person promoted is actually the supervisor's girlfriend, it will not generally be considered sexual harassment. However, if there is a pattern where workers who submit to sex with the supervisor get promoted, then sex may be considered a *condition* of the job, and it can be found to be sexual harassment under the law.

For example, in one case, a young woman worked for an equipment rental company as a forklift manager. For two years, the president of the company repeatedly asked her and other female workers to reach into the front pocket of his pants to retrieve coins. He also threw items to the ground in front of them and asked them to bend over in front of him and pick the items up. He frequently made sexual comments when referring to the women's clothing. He also told the young forklift manager, "you're a woman, what do you know," "you're a dumb ass woman," and "we need a man as the rental manager." He also told her in front of other employees and a client that they should go to a motel to negotiate her raise. (*Harris v. Forklift Sys., Inc.*, 510 U.S. 17 (1993).)

In the *Harris* case, when the president of the company told the woman that they needed to go to a motel to *negotiate* her raise, it was quid pro quo sexual harassment. The law does not require the employee to submit to the demand. The sexual advance or demand became an illegal condition of the job.

Similarly, the Supreme Court of California clarified that sexual favoritism can cause a hostile work environment. (*Miller v. Department of Corrections*, No. S114097 (July 18, 2005).) In *Miller*, two female correctional workers complained that sexual favoritism by the warden was so widespread that even though it was not directed at them, it created a hostile working environment.

The warden of the prison had affairs with three female workers. All of these workers got special treatment or promotions. Although the two plaintiffs were not subjected to sexual advances, they were denied promotions and threatened with negative consequences to their jobs if they revealed the affairs. Eventually, both plaintiffs resigned because of the favoritism. The Supreme Court of California said that the favoritism was so widespread it literally changed the work environment. More important was the recognition that both men and women could make the claim of hostile work environment where they were not the targets of the sexual advances, even though the women who did engage in the affairs did so voluntarily and welcomed the sexual relationship. The court made the point that it was not the presence of the sexual relationships that was the problem—it was the effect of those relationships on the workplace that created the hostile work environment.

Same Sex

Sexual harassment claims can be made on the basis of same-sex harassment. In *Oncale v. Sundowner Offshore Services*, 523 U.S. 75 (1998), the United States Supreme Court was faced with a case in which Joseph Oncale worked as part of an all-male crew of an oil rig. Oncale was subjected to sexual advances, threats, and even sexual assaults by his coworkers and his supervisor. Oncale complained, but nothing was done to improve the situation. Eventually, he quit to avoid being raped. Both the trial and appellate courts in that case said that the law did not protect same-sex harassment. Oncale appealed to the Supreme Court, which unanimously disagreed. Any severe and pervasive harassment based on sex is sexual harassment.

Harassment Outside of Workplace

Generally, employers are not responsible for off-hours behavior that is not work related. However, when sexual harassment takes place at a company party that the victim is expected to attend, on a roadtrip on behalf of the company, or in some other context that is work related, the question becomes whether that location can be considered part of the workplace. If so, the conduct can be considered in a sexual harassment claim.

DISCRIMINATION LAWS ARE NOT A CIVILITY CODE

While there are few bright lines in the area of sexual harassment, most cases can be determined by looking at the circumstances surrounding the conduct. Is it physical? Is it severe? Is it intended to be hurtful or disrespectful? How does the person respond to the behavior or conduct?

The Supreme Court has recently made clear that unless the conduct is physically invasive (like grabbing a breast), a victim must usually show a pattern of harassing behavior in order to demonstrate a legal claim for sexual harassment. This is because the antidiscrimination laws are not a *general civility code*. Teasing, general comments, or isolated instances of sexual conduct will not usually rise to the level of a legal case of sexual harassment. Also, flirting or isolated joking is not usually considered sufficient to show sexual harassment.

For example, it was not sexual harassment, but just *the ordinary tribulations of the workplace* where, over a period of six to seven months, a supervisor asked the plaintiff to lunch several times, told her she looked very beautiful, and put his hand on her knee one time. (*Gupta v. Florida Board of Regents*, 212 F.3d 571 (11th Cir. 2000).)

PSYCHOLOGICAL HARM

Showing that sexual harassment is so severe and pervasive that it literally changed the conditions of the job means that it either is *severe* (threats or forcible touching) or *pervasive* (a high number of times it occurred). At the same time, the Supreme Court has made clear that a victim does not have to wait until she literally suffers mental harm before she can prove a hostile environment.

For example, in *Harris v. Forklift Sys., Inc.*, the Court said that an employee who works in an environment that is poisoned with severe and pervasive sexual harassment does not have to wait until she is psychologically harmed before she can file a lawsuit under Title VII. In *Harris*, the Court found that when a female employee was continually mocked and ridiculed with dirty jokes, lewd comments, and sexual innuendo by the president of the company, the constant harassment made her job stressful and unpleasant. Therefore, she was entitled to leave and file suit before she became injured as a result. (510 U.S. 17 (1993).)

As the next chapter shows, the consequences of sexual harassment can be very serious.

chapter four:
The Impact
of Sexual Harassment

"My stomach would get sick....I had nightmares....it made my [male and female] coworkers uncomfortable...so it affected all of us."
    —comment from a respondent to a Merit Systems Protection Board survey

Sexual harassment can cause serious harm to its victims, their families, and other coworkers. Sexual harassment also has a destructive effect on an entire workplace. The victim's work performance declines as the stress of sexual harassment distracts her from work. Coworker friends become less productive, as they spend work time strategizing on ways to solve the problem. Employers are especially impacted, because every year hundreds of millions of dollars are lost in disrupted productivity. Ultimately, there is a turnover of tens of thousands of experienced female employees.

"[R]espect for women" is one of the "nonnegotiable demands of human dignity."
    —President Bush, State of the Union Speech, 2002

Job opportunities, pay, and potential for promotion are what all workers seek from employment. However, while considerable progress has been made to improve the status of women in the workplace, victims still suffer severe consequences as a result of sexual harassment. One writer has observed that:

> *[Sexual harassment] is a personal attack on women's minds and bodies, instilling fear and violating a woman's right to bodily integrity, education, and freedom of movement. It is utilized as a powerful mechanism of control and intimidation, through which women's subordinate social status is maintained. Sexual harassment frequently occurs on the street, in the workplace, in educational institutions and on public transportation. The more pernicious form, however, is sexual harassment in the workplace or in educational institutions. Sexual harassment strikes at the heart of women's economic self-sufficiency, disrupting women's earning capacity by forcing them out of the workplace or school. Women are nine times more likely than are men to leave their jobs as a result of sexual harassment.*[17]

Sexual harassment causes harm to its victims that goes far beyond the workplace. Victims suffer physical, mental, emotional, and financial losses that can all be devastating. The *National Institute for Occupational Safety and Health* (NIOSH) has reported that working women face higher risks than men from job-related stress, and one of the most *noxious* stressors is sexual harassment.

In examining why stress was such a common response to sexual harassment, one author found the following.

Despite the influx of women into the labor force, statistics show that women generally hold lower status jobs than those held by most men. They are more likely than men to be in jobs that require minimal formal education or training and are, thus, more replaceable than the men in their workplace. Therefore, there is a high probability that the man who directs his sexual attentions toward a woman has certain advantages over her. He is likely to be in a position of direct or indirect authority over her job....If she directly refuses or objects to the sexual attention, she risks job security or advancement. If she tries to ignore or politely handle it, it will continue and very likely get more intense or result in job loss anyway. The conflict created by this double bind expresses itself as mental and physical stress symptoms.[18]

Most victims experience stress-related conditions that can be traumatic. In one study, 96% of sexual harassment victims experienced emotional stress, about half suffered work performance stress, and over a third had physical stress problems. In fact, sexual harassment causes so many damaging physical, mental, and emotional effects on its victims that the American Psychiatric Association has recognized that it is a severe stressor that can contribute to posttraumatic stress disorder. Sexual harassment also affects the victims' relationships with their families, as well as friendships both inside and out of the workplace.

Research has documented that a sequence of changes occurs in victims of sexual harassment. Because sexual harassment is often based on a series of incidents, the victim may initially have thought that each incident was an isolated event and that the harassment would stop after each time. When it does not, the victim commonly feels confused or blames herself for not recognizing what was happening earlier. Next comes anxiety as the victim realizes that the harassment is continuing and wonders when it will stop. Anxiety impairs concentration, and her work responsibilities may suffer. She feels that she is being singled out, scrutinized, and targeted unfairly, yet feels trapped by the situation. She may avoid work or take leave to get away from the situation. Finally, the victim becomes angry. This may be due to a change in job, where she was forced to quit or was fired. Not surprisingly, research has shown that it is in the anger stage that most victims think about filing charges. But depression can also set in as the disappointment and frustration at the situation begins to make her feel that she may not achieve justice.

EMOTIONAL EFFECTS

Emotional trauma can be as disabling to a person as a visible, physical wound. Sexual harassment is humiliating and degrading, and can cause victims to suffer a loss of self-confidence and self-esteem. Even less severe harassment, if repeated, can have a serious, stressful effect on workers. Many cases of sexual harassment involve repeated acts, and may last one to six months or more. The workplace becomes a place to dread and work productivity suffers. One study showed that about 5% of victims quit their jobs, while 25% of victims used sick or vacation time to avoid the workplace. Even in victims who tried to ignore the harassment, productivity dropped 10%. Coworkers are also affected—simply being in the environment of harassment drops their productivity by 2%.

The emotional effect of sexual harassment also takes a toll on the desire to work at all. The victim's self-confidence is affected. She may feel incompetent and question her desire to work in that field or at all. Emotionally, victims often feel embarrassed and ashamed at being targeted for abuse. Most report being that the constant stress and tension caused them to be scared, nervous, irritable, and suffer crying spells.

In the words of one victim, "I became very nervous. It made me emotionally upset all the time. I hated to go to work. Finally, my doctor put me on tranquilizers."

Victims may feel that they do not know how to stop it or when it will end. Some may try to gain control by changing their mannerisms or dress, thinking that they, in some way, are causing the harassment.

At times, victims of harassment feel tremendous anger over their situation. As the effects of the sexual harassment are compounded over time, victims may have difficulty concentrating and feel helpless, isolated, and vulnerable. Ultimately, they may become depressed, have anxiety attacks, or even have a nervous breakdown.

In one case where a young woman was sexually harassed for a period of six weeks, she suffered severe emotional distress. She relapsed into an earlier eating disorder and substance abuse, and attempted suicide as a result of the sexual harassment. (*Schmidt v. Smith*, 684 A.2d 66 (N.J.Super. 1996).)

PHYSICAL EFFECTS

The victim may not realize it, but emotional distress can—and often does—have a direct effect on other bodily functions. Sleeplessness may lead to fatigue, which may contribute to aches, pains, or increased susceptibility to illness.

Physically, the symptoms of stress can often be seen in women whose weight fluctuates. Their stomach may be upset and they may begin vomiting or stop eating, causing weight loss. Or, they may seek comfort in food and gain considerable weight. Victims also report having heart palpitations or high blood pressure. Many are fatigued or feel exhausted constantly. Often, victims report headaches and muscle aches. Their worry and anxiety may make it hard for them to sleep or may give them nightmares. They may also have hives or experience allergic reactions. Alcohol and substance abuse have also been reported as victims attempt to numb the stress of the workplace.

ECONOMIC EFFECTS

Sexual harassment may have severe economic effects on a victim. A woman may be denied training opportunities, a promotion, or a raise. In retaliation for complaining, she may be reassigned to a difficult position or transferred away from her family and support. When a complaint is made, it may cause a division in the workplace. Certain employees may side with one party or the other. The rumor mill may escalate the situation. Many women leave their jobs every year and face unemployment. The effects of sexual harassment may follow her from the workplace, because it may have an effect on her work record and references.

Even if the worker attempts to stay on the job, sexual harassment that is severe enough to change the conditions of the work environment may make it effectively impossible to stay on the job. In effect, she may be *constructively discharged* (forced to quit by the conditions of the job), causing even more trauma and havoc.

Recognizing the terrible impact of sexual harassment on victims can help you to protect yourself from its debilitating effects and decide on a strategy that will end the harassment.

Section Two:
Employers

chapter five:
When an Employer will be Held Responsible for Sexual Harassment

Employers have a duty to protect their employees from quid pro quo or hostile work environment sexual harassment coming from supervisors, coworkers, and even outside personnel, such as contractors or customers. When they fail, they can be held responsible for sexual harassment.

Until 1998, an employer was only liable when a manager committed sexual harassment if the employer knew or should have known about it, and did nothing to correct it. However, this proved a difficult standard to meet in the case of supervisors. So, in 1998, the United States Supreme Court decided that to demonstrate the seriousness of sexual harassment, the law would hold an employer liable when its managers or supervisors are the harassers, and when the harassment results in the victim's loss of a job, or some other negative, tangible employment action, even if the company did not know about it. An employer may also be held liable for sexual harassment committed by coworkers and third parties, but there must be proof that the employer knew or should reasonably have known of the harassment, and failed to take steps to correct it.

WHO AN EMPLOYER IS

Federal law defines an *employer* as one who has fifteen or more workers, but state fair employment practice laws vary. Some states include all employers, no matter how many workers, while others include employers with more than twenty workers as the minimum number to which sexual harassment laws apply. (See Appendix C for your state laws.)

SUPERVISORS

In certain cases of sexual harassment by supervisors, the law holds an employer completely responsible, even if the employer claims that it had no knowledge of the sexual harassment. This is called *strict liability*.

In the case of *Burlington Indus., Inc. v. Ellerth*, 524 U.S. 742 (1998), the United States Supreme Court decided that a new standard of *vicarious liability* would apply when a hostile work environment is created by a supervisor's sexual harassment. *Vicarious liability* means that the supervisor is acting as the agent of the employer and can cause the employer to be held liable for the supervisor's acts.

This level of responsibility is placed on the employer because a supervisor is considered to be an *agent* of the employer. This means that he or she has the authority to make certain decisions on behalf of the employer. When the supervisor acts, it is as if the employer itself is taking the action. Because the employer gave the supervisor power, the employer is held responsible for the supervisor's sexual harassment.

Employers are strictly responsible for supervisors who commit quid pro quo sexual harassment. For example, one of the powers of a supervisor might be to recommend a raise for an employee. When a supervisor obtains sexual favors in return for that raise, the supervisor acts as the employer's agent in abusing the authority of the employer. Similarly, the employer is strictly liable when the victim submitted to the supervisor's sexual demands, and received a raise or promotion as a result. An employer will also be held strictly liable for the supervisor's hostile work environment sexual harassment if it affects a *tangible employment decision*, such as the hiring, firing, promoting, demoting, or reassigning of the victim.

Who a Supervisor Is

A *supervisor* is simply a person with authority over an employee. This can be a person's direct boss or a supervisor who has input into the decisions made about the employee. For example, the supervisor may be on the personnel team and participate in decisions about an employee's assignment within the company. Ultimately, because many companies use different titles for their managers, the decision of whether someone is a supervisor depends more on the job function than on the job title.

Sometimes a supervisor acts as if he has more power than he actually does. He may tell the target of his harassment that he can "put in a good word for her during company evaluations." Even if he does not actually have this power, if the victim reasonably believed that the harasser has the ability to recommend a tangible employment decision (like a raise), the employer will be strictly liable for the harassment. The law holds the employer responsible, because the employer put the supervisor in the position of authority. It is more fair to put the burden for the scope of that authority onto the employer than it is to require an employee to figure out what exact responsibilities a supervisor has in a tangible employment decision.

A *tangible employment decision* includes any significant change in employment status. This usually requires an official act of the employer, which will be documented in official company records. For example, a demotion is an official act of the employer and usually it results in loss of salary, wages, or benefits.

Other examples of tangible employment actions include:
- hiring and firing;
- promotion or failure to promote;
- undesirable reassignment;
- significantly more or less benefits;
- significantly more or less compensation; and,
- work assignment.

Some types of significant employment changes are obvious, like promotions, but the law also covers other, less obvious changes. For example, victims of sexual harassment have reported that upon refusal of the sexual advances of a supervisor, they were reassigned to a job with no defined responsibilities and no chance for advancement. *Warehousing* an employee is considered a tangible employment action, even if she keeps her salary and benefits. If the change merely affects the title of the position, that would not generally be enough to meet the requirement that the victim suffered a tangible employment action.

Once an employee shows that the harassment by a supervisor resulted in an actual employment action, the employer must provide a nondiscriminatory explanation. For example, if the employer shows that the reason for the action was not discriminatory, but instead was taken as an ordinary business decision (like downsizing), the victim will then have to prove that the employer's reasons are designed to hide the true discriminatory motive of sexual harassment. For example, in one case, the victim of sexual harassment was laid off because the company said it faced a significant reduction in workforce. But the evidence showed that the company's budget projected an increase in business, and no other employees were laid off. The employer's defense of *reasonable business necessity* was rejected.

THREATS, BUT NO ACTUAL EMPLOYMENT ACTION TAKEN YET

If a supervisor threatens to take a negative action, such as demotion, but does not carry out the threat, the employer may still be held responsible for sexual harassment. Similarly, a victim of hostile environment sexual harassment could be promoted, and the employer may still be held responsible for the sexual harassment. These cases, however, will be considered under a different standard.

Unlike the strict liability imposed in cases of actual employment action, the law in cases where a threatened action has not yet been taken permits an employer to completely avoid responsibility or to limit its liability. The employer must demonstrate all three of the following circumstances:

1. the employer had a sexual harassment policy;
2. effective procedures existed to address sexual harassment; and,
3. the employee failed to make a complaint.

The goal of the law is to prevent and correct sexual harassment. The best way to do this is to let an employer know about it so it can be corrected. These rules mean that an employee should report the case to his or her employer as soon as reasonably possible.

For example, a female lifeguard for the parks department of a city worked for a male supervisor, who said he would "never promote a woman." Another supervisor told her, "Date me or clean the toilets for a year." Both supervisors frequently made lewd comments about her and other female workers. They also requested sexual favors. The city had a sexual harassment policy, but it was never distributed to the lifeguards or these supervisors. The victim quit and then filed a lawsuit. The court said it was a hostile environment, and the city was liable for the actions of its supervisors because it did not distribute its sexual harassment policy. (*Faragher v. City of Boca Raton*, 524 U.S. 775 (1998).)

In another case, in which a female sales manager was sexually harassed by her supervisor's boss, the result was different. In that case, on one business trip, the boss invited her to the hotel lounge, and commented about her breasts, telling her to "loosen up" and that he "could make [her] life very hard or very easy" at the job. A few months later, when she was being reviewed for a promotion, he reached out and rubbed her knee, and said that she might not get it because she was not "loose enough." She was promoted anyway, but in promoting her, he said, "you're gonna be out there with men who work in factories, and they certainly like women with pretty butts and legs." Later, when she called with a sales request, he said he did not have time to talk unless she wanted to tell him what she was wearing. When she called back again, he denied her request, but suggested that if she wore shorter skirts, it would make her job "a whole heck of a lot easier."

She knew the company had a policy against sexual harassment, but she did not report it because under the policy, her immediate supervisor would have been required to report to her harasser. She quit and filed a lawsuit instead. The court said that there was a hostile environment, but the company was entitled to show that it had a reasonable policy, and it might be able to avoid liability or reduce damages because she never used it. (*Burlington Industries, Inc. v. Ellerth*, 524 U.S. 742 (1998).)

CONSTRUCTIVE DISCHARGE

Employees are expected to stay on the job while they follow the employer's complaint process. Sometimes the hostile work environment is so abusive that the employee resigns due to the harassment. A constructive discharge is, in effect, a firing, because the hostile work environment has forced the worker to resign. The question in these cases is, *did the working condition become so intolerable that a reasonable person in the victim's position would have felt compelled to resign?* If so, the employee has been constructively discharged.

In 2004, the United States Supreme Court said that if the abusive working environment became so intolerable that quitting was a fitting response, it was a case of a hostile work environment.

The next question regards who caused the conditions. If it was an official company act, like a demotion or extreme cut in pay, then the company will be strictly liable. If the hostile work environment was caused by coworkers or unofficial acts of a supervisor, then employers can raise a defense that it had in place reasonable corrective policies, but that the target of the harassment failed to take advantage of them. An employer will be liable if the employee is constructively discharged, unless the employer had a sexual harassment policy, effective procedures existed to address sexual harassment, and the employee failed to make a complaint. (*Pennsylvania State Police v. Suders*, 542 U.S. 129 (2004).)

THE RESPONSIBILITY OF AN EMPLOYEE TO REDUCE HARM

An employee must make an effort to use the company policy when it is reasonable to do so. This requirement does not mean that at the very first sign of sexual harassment, an employee must immediately file a formal complaint—but where it is reasonable to do so, the employee must access the company policy. Of course, if the policy is unreasonable or ineffective, the employee will not be held to task for failure to access it.

For example, if the only person an employee can report to is the very supervisor who is harassing her, it is not going to be considered a reasonable policy. Also, if the procedures require filing a certain form, but no one has even seen a copy of the form in their department, then the procedures will not be considered to be reasonable. The point is that employers should be encouraging—not discouraging—employees to report and use the process.

A Hooters restaurant manger repeatedly asked a waitress to go home or to a hotel with him, and told her that he would like to take her home and tie her up. These comments were "non-stop and they were very offensive" and made her feel "like a piece of meat, degraded, violated." He also put his hand in her shorts, pulled out her panty hose, and looked down into them. Another manager also made sexist comments, along the lines of, "if he had a wife, she would bow down to him and be subservient to him."

Hooters had a written policy against sexual harassment that was given to all waitresses, and the waitress had signed a copy of the policy, stating that she had read and understood it. However, the victim said she did not have any faith in the policy because she complained once, and the sexual harassment stopped briefly, but then continued. She did not complain again. She was awarded $25,000 actual damages and $250,000 punitive damages, but because Hooters had made a good faith effort to comply with antidiscrimination laws, her $250,000 punitive damage award was eliminated on appeal.

COWORKERS

For coworkers who are not supervisors, the majority of cases have been decided under a theory of hostile environment. A coworker usually does not have power over the plaintiff to create a quid pro quo situation. For coworkers, the employer will be held responsible for sexual harassment if the employer knew (or should have known) about the sexual harassment and failed to take immediate, reasonable steps to correct the situation.

An employer can be considered to have this knowledge in two ways:
1. actual or
2. constructive.

Actual knowledge exists:
- when the managers or supervisors know about the sexual harassment, such as when the victim files a complaint;
- if the management witnesses the harassment, such as when graffiti litters the walls or pictures are posted on bulletin boards; or,
- if other employees complain about the harassment.

Constructive knowledge means that the employer should have known. This would exist in a situation where obscene materials existed throughout the workplace. Even if the supervisors ignored the situation and the employer claimed that no one complained about sexual harassment, the employer should have known about the hostile work environment.

Even if no one complains of sexual harassment, an employer has a duty to prevent it. It does not matter that the employees are willing to accept it. Once the employer knows that a workplace is hostile, it has a duty to change the environment.

Reasonable steps to prevent or end sexual harassment include cleaning off the graffiti, sending out a memo prohibiting such conduct, and reminding employees that anyone caught doing it again will be disciplined. Then, if it happens again, the employer should be willing to discipline the culprit. The employer, in many cases, should also hold a training session, reminding employees of the harassment. These are some among many measures that an employer can take. Each measure will be examined in light of the circumstances faced by the employer.

CUSTOMERS AND OTHER NONEMPLOYEES

The last category of persons an employer may be held responsible for and who can create a hostile work environment are third parties, including vendors, contractors, clients, customers, or even members of the public. Like coworkers, if an employer knew or should have known of the conduct but failed to take immediate corrective action, it can be held liable for the hostile environment.

In one case, a female receptionist in a lobby was subjected to a dress code that required her to wear a revealing uniform. She was sexually harassed by customers and members of the public. She made numerous complaints about the uniform, which was a poncho that was so short that it revealed both sides of her thighs and buttocks. The company refused to take any action to change the uniform, and she was fired when she refused to continue to wear the outfit. The company was held responsible for the customers' sexual harassment. (*EEOC v. Sage Realty Corporation*, 507 F. Supp. 599 (S.D.N.Y. 1981).)

In another case, the dress code for waitresses at Hooters was called into question. Female employees are required to wear tight, white tops and bright orange shorts. The T-shirts have the Hooters owl eyes logo across the front, which looks strikingly similar to nipples. Hooters has been sued several times for sexual harassment by supervisors and managers. One 1993 case involving six waitresses was brought on the basis that the dress code invited customer harassment. The waitresses said that customers felt free to make sexual comments. Some were asked if they wore underwear or asked their bra size. Others were simply asked for sex. Managers told them to tolerate it. When they sued, Hooters settled the case.[19]

Of course, the level of control an employer has over customers or other third parties is an important consideration, as the next case shows. Two customers subjected a Pizza Hut waitress to two months of sexual harassment. The customers asked her personal questions, and one of them grabbed her by the hair. When she complained, instead of dealing with the unruly customers, her supervisor ordered her to *waitress*. After she returned, "the customer pulled her to him by the hair, grabbed her breast, and put his mouth on her breast." She quit, sued, and was awarded $200,000, plus her attorney's fees. (*Lockard v. Pizza Hut, Inc.*, 162 F.3d 1062 (10th Cir. 1998).)

INDIVIDUAL HARASSERS HELD RESPONSIBLE FOR THEIR HARASSMENT

Individual harassers have not often been held liable for their harassment under antidiscrimination laws. However, some states do allow suits against individual harassers, and they can be held responsible using other avenues.

Federal laws regarding sexual harassment cover *employers*, so usually, individual employees are not held responsible. The law is written this way so that an employer will not escape its responsibility by placing all the blame (and the liability) on individual employees. Otherwise, the employer would just blame the employee, fire that person, and be able to escape the responsibility for allowing sexual harassment to continue in its workplace. Some courts today, however, are willing to hold a supervisor personally responsible along with the employer. State laws vary, but some do hold supervisors personally responsible for sexual harassment.

Private lawsuits for assault, battery, intentional infliction of emotional distress, and other theories (and which of these can be joined with those for sexual harassment) are not subject to the same limitations as far as who can be sued. They can be brought against any person who committed the harassment. Also, depending on the conduct, the harasser may be charged criminally. (See Section Three of this book for more details on those options.)

chapter six:
What an Employer Should Do to Prevent Sexual Harassment

An employer should take all steps necessary to prevent sexual harassment from occurring, such as affirmatively raising the subject, expressing strong disapproval, developing appropriate sanctions, informing employees of their right to raise and how to raise the issues of harassment under Title VII, and developing methods to sensitize all concerned.

—EEOC Guidelines

All employers have a responsibility to prevent sexual harassment in the workplace. The best way for your employer to prevent sexual harassment is through strong policies and procedures that prohibit it, and education and training programs to enforce the policies. Your employer must also make sure that the policy gets out to the employees and the employees know how to use it. For more information on using a company policy, see Chapter 9 of this book.

Any employer who is serious about preventing sexual harassment in the workplace will sensitize all its employees to the issues surrounding sexual harassment. Many are adopting zero-tolerance policies, which strictly prohibit certain sexual comments or acts. In 2005, California acted to require all employers with fifty or more employees to provide training on sexual harassment.

A SEXUAL HARASSMENT POLICY

An employer should have a sexual harassment policy that clearly explains to all employees that sexual harassment will not be tolerated by any employee, supervisor, coworker, customer, contractor, or anyone else who conducts business with the employer. Strong policies encourage victims to come forward and allow the employer to take prompt action to remedy sexual harassment before it affects the entire workplace.

The policy should require any employee to report the conduct that he or she believes is sexually harassing to a supervisor or other designated employee.

The policy should:

- clearly define sexual harassment;
- include specific examples of unlawful behavior;
- make clear that the behavior need not be directed at any particular person; and,
- provide confidentiality for those who report or assist in the investigation of sexual harassment.

An employer will have to share some information during the investigation of the report, but the policy should provide that information will be shared on a need-to-know basis. The employer will keep detailed records of the reports, investigations, and outcomes of sexual harassment cases. The policy should be that records are available on the same need-to-know basis.

The policy should also:

- guarantee that there will be no retaliation against the victim or any person who reported the sexual harassment;
- provide information on what legal remedies are available, such as filing a complaint with the state or federal antidiscrimination agency;
- state that the employer is committed to making a prompt, thorough, and impartial investigation of the complaint;
- provide that the victim will get notice of the results of any investigation;
- tell violators that they will be subject to disciplinary action and what the potential sanctions are; and,
- include follow-up procedures to ensure subsequent acts of harassment or retaliation are not occurring.

Distribution

Every employee should get a copy of the policy and procedures of the employer. These will usually be in the employee handbook, but some states also require them to be posted in various areas of the workplace. If the policy is changed, a new copy should be distributed. Some employers annually send out a copy as a reminder of its policy.

COMPLAINT PROCEDURES

The EEOC requires employers to work to prevent sexual harassment. One of the best ways they can do this is by developing a clear policy against sexual harassment. The policy should define what sexual harassment is and provide specific procedures for preventing it, such as setting up regular training programs and imposing discipline for violating the policy. The policy should also make clear that retaliation for making a complaint under the policy is punishable as a separate disciplinary matter.

A sexual harassment policy must be implemented through an appropriate grievance or complaint procedure. The grievance procedure provides the actual steps for filing, investigating, and resolving reports of sexual harassment.

Reporting Methods

In order to be effective, a procedure must be usable. Procedures that encourage reporting are critical to an effective policy. The procedure should describe how the report should be made and to whom. There may be a particular form to use. The procedure should have more than one way in which a report can be made. For example, the procedure should permit a report to be:

- oral;
- written;
- in person;
- by hot line; or,
- anonymous.

The policy should also provide for the length of time within which the employer's conclusions will be made. Information on how to appeal the report should be included as well.

Time Limits

The length of time to report sexual harassment should be clearly stated in the procedures. Employers who institute unreasonably short time limits for reporting sexual harassment will be found to have an unrealistic procedure. On the other hand, employers are under a duty to promptly resolve sexual harassment, so they want employees to promptly report it.

The procedure should also specify the time line for investigating and resolving reports. Once the complaint is filed, the length of time to review records, interview witnesses, and collect other evidence should be specified. Once the investigation is con-cluded, the length of time within which a written report is due should be specified, and the time and mechanism for appeal by the person who reported the harassment or the person who is accused should be specifically provided.

Interim Measures

After a complaint is reported, and while it is being investigated, the employer has a duty to protect the victim and to prevent continued harassment or retaliation for reporting. Interim meas-ures allow the employer to temporarily correct the situation. For example, a victim can request:

- a transfer;
- a shift change;

- a new seat assignment; or,
- increased supervision or monitoring.

Interim measures will also allow the employer to temporarily suspend the person accused of harassment or remove that person from the workplace.

Investigation

Employers are required to promptly investigate whether a complaint is valid, and if it is, determine what should be the appropriate remedy. Employers may also investigate where there is no formal complaint. Usually, personnel from the human resources office are charged with initially investigating a complaint. They first look to see whether the conduct charged meets the definition of sexual harassment. They look at the conduct and also at the context to determine whether it was unwelcome. Next, the investigator will determine whether the employee considered the conduct offensive. All of the circumstances surrounding the complaint will be examined.

Conclusion

If the investigation shows that the sexual harassment occurred, the investigator will then prepare a report and notify the reporting employee. The person who has committed the sexual harassment will be notified and disciplined according to the employer's policy. Examples of measures to correct the effects of the harassment are:

- restoration of leave taken because of the harassment;
- deletion of negative evaluations in employee's personnel file that arose from the harassment;

- reinstatement;
- discipline of the harasser;
- apology by the harasser;
- monitoring treatment of the employee to ensure that she is not subjected to retaliation by the harasser or others in the workplace because of the complaint; and,
- correction of any other harm caused by the harassment (e.g., compensation for losses).

LOVE CONTRACTS

Many happy relationships and marriages come from people who meet at work. But some employers see the potential for sexual harassment in socializing. To avoid liability, they develop various policies to try to avoid lawsuits for sexual harassment, one of which is the rather silly policy of having employees sign a *love contract*.

These agreements require one employee to state that their private, sexual behavior with another employee is welcome. The contract usually asks the employee to agree to arbitration through a fair employment agency or court. Employers who offer these agreements believe that they can head off a sexual harassment complaint that arises out of a soured relationship.

Be aware that these *contracts* are not really a contract at all. They invade an employee's privacy and do not protect employees. The real goal is to shield an employer from liability. If you are asked to sign such an agreement (which may also be called a *memo of understanding*), you should consider speaking to an attorney about it.

More often, employers have policies that prohibit one spouse from supervising another. This policy usually extends to prohibit or any person from supervising someone they have an intimate relationship with.

DISCIPLINE

Most employers have general disciplinary policies, but the sexual harassment policy should include the specific potential discipline for violating the sexual harassment policy. Usually, employers will have a progressive disciplinary policy depending on the severity of the violation. For example, a reprimand may be instituted for a first-time offender in a relatively minor case, but immediate dismissal will result from more severe conduct or repeated offenses, even if of a less severe nature. The following sanctions should be included in a disciplinary policy:

- oral or written warning or reprimand;
- transfer or reassignment;
- demotion;
- reduction of wages;
- suspension;
- discharge;
- training or counseling of harasser to ensure that he or she understands why his or her conduct violated the employer's anti-harassment policy; and,
- monitoring of harasser to ensure that harassment stops.

EDUCATION AND TRAINING

The employer should provide intake and annual training for all workers on its sexual harassment policies and procedures. Managers and supervisory personnel will often be given additional training to recognize their responsibilities to the employees they supervise.

SURVEYS

Periodically, employers evaluate whether their policies and procedures are helpful to employees. They may send out surveys or questionnaires. They may also have occasional discussion sessions with employees.

Employers hold the key to preventing sexual harassment in the policies and procedures they promote in the workplace. The company policy should be more than a once-read document tucked away in an employee handbook. It should be the foundation for how the employer expects all of its employees to conduct themselves at work. The policy should form the basis for regular training and a checkpoint for discussion.

The same advice for an employee who is the target of sexual harassment can be offered to an employer—do not ignore sexual harassment, because it will not go away by itself. Employers who are diligent in monitoring the workplace for the presence of sexual harassment and who take reasonable steps to correct any complaints will not only have a more productive workplace, but also be unlikely to find themselves facing a lawsuit. It is in everyone's best interest for an employer to have a good anti-harassment policy, and to follow that policy with continuing education on a frequent basis.

Section Three:
Remedies

chapter seven:

What You Can Do about Sexual Harassment

How a person handles any crisis depends on his or her personality and the circumstances. Most harassers will continue as long as they can, and unless they quit or get transferred, the harassment is unlikely to stop. There are several strategies that can help to end this obnoxious abuse of power. Choosing the strategy that is best for you depends on the severity of the harassment and on your own circumstances.

THE DECISION TO REPORT

As shown in earlier sections of this book, sexual harassment exists in all kinds of workplaces, and can have a devastating impact on the target, coworkers, and even employers. Even so, it is hard for many women to report it and fewer still make a formal complaint. Many women do not report harassment out of fear that they will not be believed or because they think nothing can be done. Some are embarrassed or ashamed, and may think the harassment was their fault.

While society applauds the idea of a whistle-blower as a person who wants to correct injustice, many women who do report sexual harassment may be criticized and isolated at work. They may be ignored or even forced out of their jobs. Employers may not take the report seriously or may be slow to respond. In some cases, they even react in a hostile manner to these reports. They may do a cursory investigation and unfound the report, making the workplace all the more intolerable. They may decide that the target of the harassment is the real problem, and demote or move the person who filed the complaint to a dead-end position. Even if the complaint is sustained, the target of harassment may find that she is denied a promotion, raise, bonus, or other job opportunity. Later evaluations may become negative when they had been positive before the complaint. Out of frustration, the target may resign, only to find that the employer blocks unemployment compensation or creates problems with references, making it hard to obtain new employment in the field.

When you are sexually harassed at work, your choices are pretty straightforward. You can ignore it or do nothing. You can make a joke of it. You can avoid the harasser if possible. You can ask or tell the harasser to stop. You can threaten to tell someone or report the harasser. On the next page, compare two surveys of thousands of workers, the first taken in the 80s and the second in the 90s.

How Workers Respond
when Faced with Sexual Harassment

ACTION	1987 workers	1994 workers
Ignored it or did nothing	52%	44%
Avoided the harasser	43%	28%
Asked/told the harasser to stop	44%	35%
Made a joke of it	20%	15%
Threatened to tell someone	14%	10%
Reported the harasser	15%	12%
Submitted to the harassment	4%	7%

NOTE: *Employees surveyed could make more than one choice.* [20]

The above chart shows that when faced with sexual harassment, most women:

- ignored it or
- avoided the harasser or the environment.

Some were able to confront the harasser. Others joined in the joking or sexual banter to feel like they had some control over the situation. Finally—and rarely—victims threatened to report, or filed a grievance or complaint.

STRATEGIES TO STOP SEXUAL HARASSMENT

What is the best strategy to stop sexual harassment? Does the fact that most women ignored the harassment or avoided the harasser mean that these are best? Should he be confronted? While every woman must decide for herself what will work, it is important to consider the outcome of the choices made by the people who have already faced harassment. Whatever else you decide to do, make sure to document it so you can keep your options open. (see page 86.)

Ignore It

The most common response to sexual harassment is to ignore the conduct. This allows the victim to keep on working in the hope that it will *just go away*. Unfortunately, ignoring the harassment may be read by the harasser as a license to continue. In the harasser's mind, the harassment has not achieved the desired effect unless the victim acknowledges it. The harasser may become bolder or intensify his efforts. Ignoring sexual harassment will rarely stop it.

Additionally, if you decide to complain later, the law may be tougher on you. One of the required elements of a sexual harassment claim is that the conduct was unwelcome. Even if you are not ready yet to confront the harasser or report the harassment, make sure you document it. (see page 86.)

Deny It

Many women simply deny that what is happening is sexual harassment. The notion that *this cannot be happening* or *he was just kidding* helps to retain the belief that you have control over your work environment. Some victims challenge their own feelings by minimizing what is happening and thinking that it was not that serious. Others discount their experience, thinking, *I am imagining things* or *I am overreacting*. While denial is a protective strategy, the harasser has time to continue and often escalate his behavior.

Avoid It

When denial becomes impossible, the victim may question if she is somehow at fault. She may change her appearance or dress in an effort to end the harassment. She may avoid being near the harasser whenever possible. None of these things will end the harassment, because the victim is not the cause of the harassment.

It is common for victims to take sick or vacation leave. They may request transfers or reassignments, or even quit to avoid the harassment. While leaving the workplace will remove the victim from the harassment, loss of sick or vacation leave—and certainly loss of a job—are a high price to pay to end the harassment. Sometimes, especially if there has been a past relationship, the harasser knows where the victim lives and continues his conduct outside of the workplace.

Join It

Some victims join in the workplace bantering, using vulgar language and acting in a sexualized manner. This is one way to live the illusion that, by becoming *one of the guys*, she will not be harassed further. However, while victims perceive joining in as a way of controlling or defusing the harassment, courts see it as contributing to the sexual conduct in the workplace, and may decide that the behavior was *welcomed* because of the victim's response. Also, going along with the harassment is the least effective thing that could have been done. In fact, the harassment usually gets worse.

Confront It

Only about one-third of women who are sexually harassed ask or tell the harasser to stop his conduct, yet this is the most effective strategy to ending the harassment. Try to gain the support of your friends in the workplace to also put pressure on the harasser to stop his conduct. Ask your employer to set up training about sexual harassment.

If you are not at risk of harm, you can say one of the following.
- "Your conduct is not acceptable."
- "You are not funny."
- "Your behavior is hurtful."
- "It is not a joke."
- "It is degrading."
- "Stop it!"

Speak firmly and with conviction. It is important to note that it can be helpful under the law that you let the harasser know that his conduct is unwelcome.

It may be that the harasser is a beginner or just a clod and totally insensitive. It is possible that the harasser does not realize the behavior is offensive. Your clear words will put the harasser on notice that his comments, jokes, conduct, or innuendo is simply not appropriate. Sometimes, if it is a less severe form of harassment or a beginning harasser, a clear, direct statement from you to stop may be all that is needed to end the behavior.

If it is too stressful to talk to the person who is harassing you, write a letter. In the letter, clearly state the behavior that is offensive to you. For example, write, "Several times you have stared at me and followed me around the office. You have put your hands on my shoulders to give me a 'massage.' You even suggested that I could 'get ahead' in the company if I went to a motel with you." Include dates and locations of this conduct.

In writing the letter, take time to create drafts so that it says exactly what you want it to say. If necessary, write more than one draft. Feel free to throw away old copies until the letter reflects your goal in writing it. Keep the letter on a professional level. Tell the harasser to stop. Tell him that the conduct makes you feel uncomfortable or threatened. Finally, tell him what solution you seek. For example, if you feel you cannot work with the harasser any longer, you might write, "I cannot work effectively under these circumstances, and therefore seek to be reassigned." You might also indicate, "in the future, please keep the work relationship on a more professional level."

Keep proof that you sent the letter. Make sure to keep a copy of the letter for later use at a more formal proceeding, if necessary.

Report It

Historically, few victims report the harassment to their employer. Few—maybe as low as 5–10%—choose to file a complaint with an outside agency. Why do victims not report harassment? They believe that others will not take it seriously. Some fear what would happen to them at work if they reported it. They are embarrassed at the notion of reporting harassment and fear retaliation at the workplace. Some believe that nothing could be done. Others think they would be blamed or that outsiders would not believe them. Some women do not report because they do not wish to hurt the person who is harassing them. Yet, when women do report sexual harassment, the majority of the time, the situation improves.

Most employers have policies addressing sexual harassment, and may allow informal and formal complaints. You may also choose to file a complaint with the EEOC or your state fair employment practice agency. These options are detailed in Chapter 10 of this book.

Whatever Else You Do— Document the Harassment

Although confronting the harasser or reporting the harassment is the most effective way to stop it, be sure to keep a record of every instance of the harassment while you are deciding on your best strategy.

Take good notes of every incident of harassment and keep them in a protected place away from your workplace. Use a notebook or diary. Make sure you document all the following information.

- *Who was present?* Always list who was there. Besides you and the harasser, who heard or saw the harassment? Write down complete names whenever possible.
- *What happened?* Record the comments, words, or jokes. Describe exactly what the conduct was. Include any contextual information, such as what happened just before or after that relates to the conduct or words.
- *When did it happen?* Include the time and date.

- *Where did it happen?* Make sure you record the exact room or location. If harassment happens outside the workplace, document that also.

Make sure you also document how each incident affected you. Keep copies of any receipts for medical care or intervention. Also, be sure to get contact information, if possible, on the coworkers or others who saw the incident in case you need to contact them later.

The form on the following page may be useful as you document the incidents of sexual harassment.

SEXUAL HARASSMENT INCIDENT FORM

Date: _____

Time: _____

Location: _____

People present:

_____

_____

Specific statements or conduct that occurred:

_____

_____

_____

_____

_____

_____

_____

_____

_____

_____

_____

_____

_____

Who else saw or heard the statements or conduct?

_____

_____

If so, what did they say or do?

_____

_____

_____

How did the statements or conduct affect you?

_____

_____

_____

_____

_____

_____

_____

_____

_____

_____

Attach any documents, including letters, notes, forms, emails, etc. (originals if possible), to this form.

Collect Important Documents

From the earliest point that you recognize the conduct as sexually harassing, be sure to keep originals (or copies) of all documents relating to your employer and your employment. These can help document evidence of harassment.

Is there a picture, photo, diagram, or drawing of the harassment? Is there a note or letter? Is there an email? If possible, get the exact item or photo, or print a copy, to keep with your documents for future use, if necessary. It may also be useful to take pictures of your workplace to show your proximity to a harasser or to show what the graffiti on the wall looked like.

Other copies to keep include relevant:
- work evaluations (good and bad);
- company handbooks or policies;
- job attendance, assignments, and proof of completion;
- company memos, newsletters, or bulletins; and,
- official correspondence from your employer.

Every worker who is being harassed must decide whether and when to report. Some survive by waiting out minor harassment when the harasser moves on to a new target or workplace. Others, when faced with more threatening behavior, decide to reach out for help in assessing their options. Whatever you decide, be sure to reach out to family, friends, and coworkers. You may learn that you are not alone in experiencing sexual harassment. You may even learn that the same harasser has done this in the past or is harassing another worker.

REPORTING OPTIONS

Perhaps the best news is that in studies of women who filed complaints of sexual harassment, nearly all were able to rebuild their working careers. From trauma came survival, and a stronger worker emerged.

If you decide that reporting is the best option for you, consider the policies and procedures your workplace provides. To decide on who to report to and how to follow up on a complaint, one must know what options are available. Other chapters in this book explain more about company policies, procedures, mediation, agency complaint filings, time limits, and procedures. Questions to ask include the following.

- To whom do you report complaints of harassment in the company?
- What is the procedure for responding to those complaints?
- If you are a member of a union, what is its policy?
- Is there an opportunity for mediation or arbitration to settle the differences?
- How do you file a complaint with the local, state, or federal agency?
- What is the time limit for doing so?
- What are the procedures of this agency?
- What are the remedies available?

chapter eight:
Remedies for Sexual Harassment

The remedies for sexual harassment may be informal or formal. Employer remedies may include reinstatement, promotion, back pay, and other types of solutions that resolve the complaint. These remedies will be found in your employee handbook or manual. Federal, state, and local laws also provide for remedies.

REMEDIES

If an employer is held responsible for sexual harassment, the plaintiff is entitled to be restored to the position she would have been in before the harassment. These are called *make whole* remedies. The plaintiff may also be entitled to compensatory and punitive damages, and attorney's fees and costs. Also, the court may order the employer to take certain actions to end sexual harassment. Remedies granted by a court will be designed to address the facts of the case presented.

Make Whole Remedies

Make whole remedies are designed to restore employment losses due to the harassment. These can include:

- back pay;
- hiring;
- promotion;
- reinstatement; and,
- front pay.

Back Pay

This remedy can be ordered to restore lost wages, overtime, a shift pay differential, or other lost benefits, such as vacation or sick leave, pension, retirement, profit sharing, or other fringe benefits, like medical and life insurance. The law allows back pay for up to two years prior to filing a charge with the EEOC. Back pay will terminate with the entry of the judgment in the sexual harassment case. The plaintiff does have a duty to *mitigate*. This means that the victim must actively seek to be reemployed at a comparable income, and if so, that amount will be deducted from the back pay awarded.

Hiring, Promotion, and Reinstatement

The plaintiff can be hired on the terms and with the same seniority she would have had if she had been hired at the time of the sexual harassment. The victim may also be reinstated to the position that the sexual harassment kept her from being promoted to, with all the benefits accruing from the time she should have been promoted. Also, a court can order that all negative evaluations be removed from her personnel file.

Front Pay

Sometimes reinstatement is not possible, such as when the job no longer exists or when it is not feasible to put the plaintiff into a particular position. If it would be inappropriate to return to her job, *front pay* for a certain length of time can be ordered. Front pay is like back pay, except that it applies to the future. It includes future salary or wages and benefits that she would have earned had she been returned to the position. Front pay will be ordered only until the time it is estimated that the plaintiff would get comparable work.

Injunctive Relief

The ability of a court to order a company to do or to stop doing something is especially important in hostile environment cases. For example, a court can order the company to cease the sexually harassing conduct. It can also order the company to provide training and educational programs to prevent sexual harassment. A court may also order the company to adopt, implement, and enforce policies and procedures for the prevention and control of sexual harassment.

Attorney's Fees and Costs

Plaintiffs who win their Title VII suit can also recover attorneys' fees, expert witness fees, and court costs.

DAMAGES AND THE CIVIL RIGHTS ACT OF 1991

A plaintiff who files a lawsuit is entitled to various remedies for her injuries. In addition to the remedies already discussed, a plaintiff is entitled to money damages for sexual harassment. As it was initially passed in 1964, Title VII only provided that victims of sexual harassment could be reinstated to their jobs, and collect back pay and lost earnings if they proved their case. But a victim of sexual harassment was not permitted to recover for pain and suffering.

Compensatory Damages

In 1991, after the Anita Hill case, the United States Congress passed amendments to Title VII to allow sexual harassment victims to request a jury trial to recover money damages as compensation for their injuries. The compensation can include future money damages, as well as recovery for emotional pain and suffering.

Punitive Damages

If there is intentional or reckless discrimination by a private employer, the sexual harassment victim can also seek punitive damages. Punitive damages are not available against state or local governments. This type of damage award is designed to punish an employer who intentionally caused harm, was reckless, or acted with *callous indifference* to the victim's harassment.

One court identified the following factors as relevant to imposition of the punitive damage consideration.

- How reprehensible was the conduct?
- What are the potential civil penalties?
- Does the award serve the future goal of deterrence?

Damage Cap

The 1991 amendment expanding the right to damages, however, provides for a combined compensatory and punitive damage cap, depending on the number of employees at the workplace. For example, the maximum a company employing fifteen to one hundred employees could be sued for is $50,000. Employers with 101–200 employees can face up to $100,000. For 201–500 employees, it is $200,000. And, for companies with 501 or more, the cap is $300,000.

INSTITUTIONAL REMEDIES

In addition to individual remedies, employers may be required by federal, state, or local law to undertake corrective measures to prevent sexual harassment from continuing or occurring in the future.

An employer may be required to post notices to all employees, addressing specific charges and informing employees of their right to a workplace free of sexual harassment. For example, an employer may be required to provide training for all its employees on sexual harassment. Additionally, the employer may be required to correct the reason that permitted the sexual harassment to exist to reduce the chance that it will reoccur. For example, an employer may be required to increase the number of women in management or in representative positions.

Often employers will settle claims, and these reforms will be a part of the settlement process. In 1999, when the Ford Company settled a class action involving sexual harassment in its assembly plants, it agreed to pay $10 million to provide sexual harassment training to all its employees. It also agreed to establish an independent monitor to oversee the process of implementing its reforms.

Smaller businesses can take more informal measures to prevent future cases of sexual harassment. For example, EEOC guidelines suggest that a small business employer can tell the employees at staff meetings that harassment is prohibited, that employees should report such conduct promptly, and that a complaint can be brought immediately to the higher-ups. If the business conducts a prompt, thorough, and impartial investigation of any complaint that arises, and undertakes swift and appropriate corrective action, it will have fulfilled its responsibility to effectively prevent and correct harassment.

chapter nine:
How to Use
the Company Process

You may have initially tried ignoring the sexual harassment, wishing it would go away, but it has not. You may have tried telling the harasser to stop. You may have engaged coworkers to help you by putting pressure on the harasser to stop. For all your actions, the harassment has not stopped. You have come to the conclusion that it is time to report your sexual harassment to your employer.

You have learned that your employer has a policy prohibiting sexual harassment in the workplace. You must read it and the procedures that implement the policy. It is especially important to understand the process you will be facing as you report sexual harassment to your employer. What follows is a typical process that employers engage in when responding to sexual harassment. However, every employer is free to develop individualized policies and procedures that address sexual harassment.

For example, most have fairly short time lines for reporting and investigating a complaint. Your employer has strong reasons to promptly investigate sexual harassment according to its policies.

But recognize that while your employer is trying to promptly resolve your complaint, it will also be developing a record for defenses that it might later raise should you make a complaint to an outside agency. One of those defenses might be your failure to promptly access the employer's sexual harassment report and investigation procedures.

PRELIMINARY CONSIDERATIONS

If you are a union member, be sure to report the harassment to your union steward, who can offer support for your report. According to the *National Labor Relations Act*, unions must represent and aid their members in stopping sexual harassment. You may wish to have a union representative or an attorney present during some of the proceedings. While the employer may do an excellent job of responding to your report, at this point you should consider talking to an attorney regarding your options. See Chapter 14 for information on how to find a lawyer.

KEEP RECORDS

Throughout the grievance or complaint process, you should keep good records of your contacts with your employer. Include the same kinds of information you are documenting regarding the actual incidents of sexual harassment. For example, for each telephone or in-person contact you have with your company about sexual harassment, you should document:

- date;
- time;
- location;

- who was present; and,
- what exactly was discussed.

You may wish to use the Sexual Harassment Incident Form from Chapter 7, on page 88.

This way, if your employer does not resolve your complaint satisfactorily, you will have good notes to use if you decide to take your complaint to an outside agency or to court.

THE REPORT OF SEXUAL HARASSMENT

The nature of sexual harassment is necessarily disturbing and distressing, but in preparing to make your report, you must carefully consider the facts that you will include. Set aside some time away from work when you can think quietly. Before you make your report, sit down and make an outline of the incidents you wish to report. Be sure to include relevant facts, such as:

- the specific conduct or acts;
- how they were unwelcome to you;
- what the impact has been;
- when the conduct occurred;
- what supporting information you have;
- who else was present;
- who would have information about the incidents;
- why you think they have information to share; and,
- documents or materials that support your report, such as letters, pictures, or drawings.

NOTE: *Before you provide any materials to your employer, make sure that you make copies for yourself. Keep your copies in a secure place outside of the workplace.*

Your employer may have a form for you to fill out. If one exists, it will usually be found in the employee handbook. If no form exists, contact one of the designated people listed in your employer's policies and procedures to initiate the complaint when you are prepared.

INVESTIGATION OF THE REPORT

Your employer will use the company's process as a guide to conducting the investigation. (See Chapter 9 for the typical parts of an employer's policies and procedures for responding to sexual harassment.) The investigation should begin promptly after the complaint is made. This may mean that day or within a few days.

In investigating a complaint of sexual harassment, employers will:

- question both parties in detail;
- seek supporting information from others; and,
- obtain various records, like personnel files or work logs.

Investigator

Your employer's policy will determine who investigates complaints of sexual harassment. An investigator might be:

- a human resource employee;
- a personnel manager;
- a consultant;
- an outside agency; or,
- a lawyer.

Whoever the investigator is, the goal of this person should be to impartially gather all the relevant evidence to determine whether a claim of sexual harassment can be substantiated, and to make recommendations about resolving the report.

The investigator should have special training both in the law and employer responsibilities regarding sexual harassment. The investigator may meet with you and others several times (if necessary) over the course of the investigation to gather information. Then, the investigator will write a report and come to a conclusion that resolves the complaint and makes recommendations to the employer. Afterward, the investigator (and sometimes a designated supervisor) will meet separately with you and the person who has been accused of harassment to explain your employer's resolution of the complaint. The investigator will also explain to both parties that regardless of whether the complaint has been sustained or not, retaliation for making a good faith complaint is prohibited and can result in a separate investigation and separate remedies.

Interview of Victim

The first thing the interviewer will likely do when you report sexual harassment is speak to you. The interview will take place in a private setting. If your employer has no form, the interviewer will document the initial report for the company records, because it is important under the law for an employer to show that it promptly responded to the complaint.

The interviewer should begin by explaining how your employer handles a report of sexual harassment and going over the company's policy. The employer's policy with respect to confidentiality should also be explained.

After the introductory material is covered, the investigator will conduct an interview. The interviewer may choose to let you go through the report once without interruptions, and then ask questions on the second time through. The interviewer may ask several questions on each point before proceeding, but you should be the one to provide the facts and details. Do not hesitate to correct the interviewer if he or she repeats any wrong or misunderstood information as part of a question.

While you are telling your experience of the harassment, the interviewer is listening and considering your words. Your credibility is being evaluated and the believability of your story is being weighed. Although talking about the sexual harassment may be stressful, you want to avoid rambling or giving a statement that is totally disorganized. Pace yourself, and if you feel that you are getting too agitated or upset, ask for a break, get a drink of water, and count to ten. It also helps to have some outline or guide to follow.

The interviewer needs to get a complete statement from you and should be taking notes; some interviewers ask permission to tape your statement to be sure it is accurate. After your words are recorded on paper, you should be given an opportunity to look over your statement and make any corrections to it. You may also be asked to sign it.

The questions you will be asked depend on your situation, but will generally cover issues that establish whether the elements of sexual harassment are present, how the conduct was unwelcome to you, and the impact it had on you and others in the workplace. After a series of introductory questions that establish your employment location and job responsibilities, the interviewer will likely cover the areas discussed on the next few pages.

The Harasser

These questions are designed to establish the name or identity of the person being accused of harassment, as well as the position that person holds with the employer. It is also important to know what kind of working relationship you have with this person, whether you had a relationship in the past, and if so, how it ended. Questions will include the following.

- Who committed the sexual acts or conduct?
- What is this person's position in the company?
- What kind of working relationship do you have with this person?
- Do you socialize or see each other outside of work?

The Sexual Advances or Conduct

Your employer needs to establish the kind and level of company violation that is being reported. Is it the quid pro quo type of sexual harassment? Is it a hostile work environment? If it is a hostile work environment, what is the frequency and severity of the conduct?

The elements of sexual harassment will be established through questions such as the following.

- What exactly occurred?
- When did it occur?
- Where did it occur?
- How often did it occur?
- Is it still ongoing?

The Impact on You

It is important to know what kind of impact the sexual harassment is having on you and your coworkers. These questions are designed to ask about your immediate impact, but also to determine how the sexual advances or conduct is impacting you as a worker and the workplace as a whole. These questions will likely include some of the following.

- How did it affect you at that time?
- What did you do in response?
- How has the harassment impacted you personally?
- Has your job been affected in any way?

Supportive Evidence

An employer will seek as much relevant information as is reasonable, given the timeline for investigating the report of sexual harassment. You will be asked if anyone else or anything else can provide information in questions like the following.

- Are there any persons who have relevant information?
- Was anyone present when the incident occurred?
- Did you tell anyone about it?
- Did anyone see you immediately afterward?
- Did the person who harassed you harass anyone else?
- Do you know whether anyone complained about harassment by that person?
- Are there any notes, physical evidence, or other documentation regarding the incident?

Your Wishes

Part of your employer's duty is to promptly address sexual harassment. Interim measures should be appropriate to your needs in the workplace. For example, you may request to be transferred or moved, or may ask for the harasser to be moved, if that is more appropriate. The employer should try to accommodate your request within the limits of its policies. Be aware that you are protected from retaliation, and should not be transferred or moved without your consent on the basis that you made the report of sexual harassment. Be sure to tell the investigator:

- how you would like to see the situation resolved;
- whether you feel secure in your work location; and,
- what would be reasonable for you while the investigation is going on.

Other Information

An interviewer should give you several chances during the interview to provide additional information as the telling of your experiences triggers your memory. Certainly, at the end of the interview there will be some general questions for this purpose. Also, you may recall more information after leaving the interview. You should contact the interviewer with any additional information. The following questions will generally be asked.

- Do you know of any other relevant information?
- Is there anyone else the investigator should talk to?

At the end of the interview, the investigator should remind you of the timelines for the investigative process and let you know the next steps that your employer will be taking. The employer will question other people you identified, and should explain to you what the company policy on confidentiality is in regard to these persons. For example, if you identified a coworker as being present for one of the incidents, the investigator will question him or her about the incident, but will not likely share information about other incidents you described unless you indicated that he or she was present for those also.

The interviewer should close the interview by reiterating your right to be protected against harassment in retaliation for making the complaint. The investigator should also tell you that the person you have identified as the harasser will be told not to engage in any kind of retaliation as a result of your complaint.

Interviewing the Person Accused of Harassment

If you identified a specific person as your harasser, that person will be interviewed and given an opportunity to answer your report. The investigator should remain neutral. Do not be surprised if the accused harasser denies your charge regardless of the proof you have offered. After determining how the person knows you and what his or her relationship is to you, questions to the person accused of harassment may include the following.

- What is your response to the complaint?
- What happened on that day?
- Why do you think the person making the report would make such a complaint?
- Why would she misunderstand you?
- Why would she lie?
- Is there anyone who can provide support for your answers?
- Who else might have relevant information?
- Are there any notes or other documentation regarding the incident?
- Do you know of any other relevant information?

Just as in your interview, the investigator will tell the person accused of harassment that retaliation will not be permitted, and that it can serve as the basis for a separate investigation and separate sanction, even if the original complaint of sexual harassment is not sufficiently proven.

Seeking Support

The investigator will also search for evidence that supports the statements from both you and the person who is accused of harassment. The employer may examine your and the harasser's personnel files to determine if there have been any prior complaints or work issues related to your complaint. The employer will also seek out other victims that may exist. You or the accused harasser may also have identified various non-employees, and given permission to your employer to contact them for additional information. For example, you may have given permission to obtain medical records to document your absenteeism due to stress-related illnesses.

Your coworkers will be interviewed, as well as any supervisors who may have contact with you. The employer will ask about the specific conduct if you identified them as witnesses. These persons may also be asked about your demeanor and the demeanor of the harasser. Others who have been identified as having some relevant information will also be questioned. Employers will often ask the following questions of them.

- What did you see or hear?
- When did this occur?
- What was the behavior of the person accused toward the complainant and others in the workplace?
- What did the complainant say about the incident?
- When did he or she tell you this?
- Do you know of any other relevant information?
- Is there any other person who has relevant information?

The Investigator's Report of Conclusions

Once all of the necessary persons have been interviewed and all of the relevant material has been examined, the investigator will come to a conclusion on whether there is a reasonable basis to believe that sexual harassment occurred. Employers are free to use different terms in their policies, but there are generally three categories of conclusions to a sexual harassment complaint:

1. *sustained* (has sufficient evidence);
2. *unfounded* (found to be untrue); or,
3. *unsubstantiated* (does not have sufficient evidence).

The investigator will weigh the credibility of the witnesses, the consistency of the statements, and the existence of any documents or material that has been provided or reviewed against the elements of a sexual harassment complaint. No single statement or item will usually be conclusive. Instead, it is the totality of the circumstances that are considered when making a report.

EMPLOYER'S RESPONSE

Regardless of the outcome of the individual complaint, if the harassment involved a hostile work environment claim or there is a concern that others in the workplace were affected, your employer may:

- send a reminder to all employees about the seriousness of sexual harassment complaints or
- set up a training for employees in your work location or throughout the employer's facility.

SUSTAINED REPORT

If the investigator concludes that the evidence in your case demonstrates that sexual harassment occurred, the investigator then recommends sanctions or turns it over to the appropriate supervisor to do so. Your employer will look to its policies to determine what sanctions to impose against the offender and what remedies are appropriate for you. For example, if the harasser is a first-time offender, and the conduct involved language or pictures, the policy may call for a warning or suspension. If the conduct involved assault, however, the report should result in the harasser being fired. You will be informed of your employer's actions.

If, as a result of the harassment, you were denied a job benefit (such as a raise or a transfer) or experienced some negative event (such as being disciplined or having a negative evaluation), your employer will also attempt to remedy the situation. Your raise should be retroactive, any negative evaluation should be removed from your personnel file, and you should be returned to the position you would have been in except for the harassment.

UNFOUNDED REPORT

Although it is rare, an intentionally false complaint of sexual harassment is occasionally made. If your employer determines that your complaint was made in *bad faith*, that is, intentionally false, your employer could discipline you for dishonesty according to its policies. However, your employer must be very careful not to engage in what might appear to be retaliation to avoid being held responsible for committing a separate violation under federal or state laws.

UNSUBSTANTIATED REPORT

When there are key inconsistencies in the statements gathered that cannot be resolved, the employer may be unable to find sufficient support for your complaint to substantiate it. If your employer determines there is not enough evidence to sustain the complaint, it will inform you and the accused harasser of its decision.

MONITORING

If the complaint is substantiated, it is likely that the employer will keep a file open to monitor the situation for some period of time. The employer may also periodically check with you to see if there are any more incidents or problems. Even if your employer finds the complaint unsubstantiated or unproven, it may increase training or monitoring of the workplace in an effort to prevent any future sexual harassment or retaliatory conduct.

EMPLOYER RECORDS

Whatever the resolution of your report, your employer will keep a written record of your complaint, the steps taken in the investigation, and the conclusions of the report.

IF THE HARASSMENT CONTINUES

Once you have filed a complaint, you must notify your employer immediately if there is any further harassment. For example, any material negative change in your employment status may be considered retaliation for filing the complaint and can be the subject of separate disciplinary action by the company.

IF YOU DECIDE TO DROP THE COMPLAINT

An employer who has notice of sexual harassment in the workplace is required to promptly investigate and respond to it. While you may decide you do not wish to proceed on your complaint, your employer cannot simply stop its investigation. It must continue and seek to resolve the report under the law.

DISAGREEING WITH
THE SANCTIONS IMPOSED

While you will be asked what you think would the best resolution to your complaint, it is the employer—based on the policies it has—that will decide what the appropriate remedy will be.

IF YOU ARE NOT SATISFIED
WITH THE RESOLUTION

You are entitled to turn to the legal system when you have been sexually harassed. Certainly, if your employer does not resolve the situation reasonably, you may file a complaint with the federal EEOC or your state fair employment practice agency, or you may file a private lawsuit. Information about your legal options can be found in Chapter 10 of this book.

chapter ten:
Filing a Complaint with the EEOC or Your State FEPA

In most cases, before you can turn to the courts for recovery for sexual harassment, you must file a complaint with the appropriate federal, state, or local fair employment agency. On the federal level, for employers with fifteen or more employees, this is the *Equal Employment Opportunity Commission* (EEOC). States that have antidiscrimination laws have an equivalent agency called the *Fair Employment Practice Agency* (FEPA). Some municipalities have also passed ordinances prohibiting sexual harassment. These cities also have agencies designed to implement their ordinances. Federal law does not apply to employers with less than fifteen employees, but state and local laws may apply to smaller employers. Find more information about the EEOC and your state's agency in Appendices A and C, respectively.

THE EQUAL EMPLOYMENT OPPORTUNITY COMMISSION

The EEOC is the federal agency charged with enforcing federal sexual harassment laws. Federal courts rely on EEOC guidelines in interpreting Title VII of the Civil Rights Act. The EEOC is very active in enforcing sexual harassment laws. The EEOC has obtained hundreds of millions of dollars in benefits for victims through its enforcement efforts.

National Enforcement Plan

The number of cases of sexual harassment reported to the EEOC has tripled over the last decade. At any given time, it may have about 80,000 pending cases. Struggling with the increased volume of cases, in 1996 the EEOC developed a plan that prioritizes three types of cases:

1. cases in which the potential impact goes beyond the parties;
2. cases that can develop the law; and,
3. cases that affect the EEOC process.

This means that the EEOC will often focus its resources on larger cases. The EEOC can and does file class action suits involving numerous women at the same company who complain of sexual harassment. In the past few years, the EEOC has settled a number of big sexual harassment and retaliation cases.

- $34 million with Mitsubishi Motor Manufacturing of America for three to four hundred female employees.
- $10 million with Astra USA for eighty to one hundred female victims.
- $8 million with Ford Motor Company for its female workers.
- $3.2 million with Tyson Foods, Inc.
- $2.6 million settlement with Sidney Frank Importers and All State Promotions for over one hundred female employees in New York State.

- $1.9 million with Long Prairie Packing, a Minnesota-based meat packing company, for sexually harassed male workers.
- $1.85 million with lettuce grower/distributor Tanimura & Antle, Inc. for a quid pro quo and retaliation case.
- $1.3 million settlement with Foster Wheeler Constructors, Inc. for racist and sexist graffiti at a construction site in Illinois.
- $1 million with Grace Culinary Systems and Townsend Culinary for egregious sexual harassment against twenty-two Hispanic female workers who were recent immigrants in low-wage jobs at a Maryland food processing plant.
- $500,000 with Burt Chevrolet and LGC Management in Colorado for ten former salesmen harassed by male managers.

Even if your case does not fit one of the priority categories, a charge must be filed with the EEOC. Smaller cases or cases that do not fit the priority plan may be referred to mediation, if the parties agree to it, in an effort to reach an early settlement.

Filing

A charge may be filed by mail or in person at the nearest EEOC office. The name of the victim in an EEOC claim may be kept confidential. (See Appendix A for contact information.)

Form

The EEOC has a form for filing the charge. It can be obtained at any EEOC office. It requires your name, address, and telephone number, as well as the name, address, telephone number, and number of employees of your employer. A brief description of the sexual harassment, including the dates of the incidents, must be provided.

Time Limits

There are short time limits for filing a charge of sexual harassment. A charge must be filed with the EEOC within the one hundred eighty days from the date of the last incident of sexual harassment. This means the date of the harassment and not the date on which your employer completed its investigation of your complaint. The one-hundred-eighty-day filing deadline is extended to three hundred days if your state or municipality has a fair employment practices act. (See Appendix C for state-specific information.) There are few situations in which the timeline may be extended, but if you are close, be sure to file your charge or contact an attorney immediately for review of your time to file.

Classification of Charge

Once your employer is notified, the EEOC may classify your charge as one of priority investigation if the initial facts appear to support a violation of law. When the evidence is less strong, your charge may be assigned for a follow up investigation to determine whether it is likely that a violation has occurred.

Dismissal of Case

The EEOC may decide to dismiss your charge if it is unable to determine that there has been a violation of the law. But even if your charge is dismissed, a *right to sue* letter is issued, which gives you ninety days in which to file a private lawsuit. (See Chapter 11 for information on filing private lawsuits.)

Investigation

In investigating a charge, the EEOC may make written requests for information, interview people, review documents, and as needed, visit the facility where the alleged discrimination occurred. When the investigation is complete, the EEOC will discuss the evidence with you and the employer, as appropriate.

Settlement

The EEOC can seek to settle a charge at any stage of the investigation if you and the employer agree. If the case cannot be settled, the investigation will continue.

Mediation

If the parties both agree, *mediation* is an informal process where you and your employer agree to settle the issues. The EEOC currently refers about 10,000 cases every year to mediation. In the process of mediation, a neutral third party will meet with the parties to negotiate a resolution. The EEOC notes the following.

Mediation gives the parties the opportunity to discuss the issues raised in the charge, clear up misunderstandings, determine the underlying interests or concerns, find areas of agreement and, ultimately, to incorporate those areas of agreements into resolutions.

The EEOC's mediation program is free, and the process is fairly short. Most mediation sessions are completed in a single visit in just a few hours. If mediation fails to resolve the case, the EEOC will proceed to investigate the case.

Sustaining a Case

If the EEOC finds evidence that you have been sexually harassed, it may use the remedies in Title VII to settle your case whenever possible. If your case is not resolved by the EEOC, it will give permission for the case to be taken to court in a private lawsuit by issuing a *right to sue* letter within ninety days. (See Chapter 11 of this book for information on filing a private lawsuit.)

Determination of Insufficient Evidence

If the EEOC does not have enough evidence, it will issue a determination that says, "Based on the Commission's investigation, the Commission is unable to conclude that the information obtained establishes violations of the statutes."

STATE AND LOCAL FAIR EMPLOYMENT AGENCIES

Like the federal law, most states provide that a complaint must be filed under the state fair employment practice law before filing with the courts. Many states and localities have antidiscrimination laws, as well as agencies responsible for enforcing those laws (called the *fair employment practices agencies* (FEPAs)).

Through the use of *work-sharing agreements*, the EEOC and the FEPAs avoid duplication of effort, while at the same time ensuring that a charging party's rights are protected under both federal and state law.

If a charge is filed with a FEPA and is also covered by federal law, the FEPA *dual files* the charge with the EEOC to protect federal rights. The charge usually will be retained by the FEPA for handling. If a charge is filed with the EEOC and also is covered by state or local law, the EEOC dual files the charge with the state or local FEPA, and ordinarily retains the charge for handling.

The procedures vary under state laws. Many follow the general procedures outlined above for the EEOC. Your state FEPA can provide you with the exact procedures for your state. A listing of your state law and agencies with contact information is found in Appendix C.

NOTE: *Unless your case is settled at the agency level, you have a right to pursue your federal and state rights by filing a private lawsuit. (See Chapter 11 for more information about lawsuits.)*

chapter eleven:
Filing a Lawsuit

What follows is an overview of the various methods by which a
sexual harassment suit can be filed. Because of the complexity
of these suits, and because employers will have attorneys, you
should consult with an attorney about the procedures involved
given your facts and circumstances. Remember that a court can
order an attorney's fee to be paid by the employer. A court may
appoint an attorney in a Title VII case based on your ability to
pay, the merits of the case, and your capacity to present your
own case. (See Chapter 14 on the role of an attorney.)

Sexual harassment can become the subject of a private civil lawsuit in one of three ways.

1. It can be filed as a federal sexual harassment suit
   under Title VII.
2. It can be filed as a violation of state fair employment
   practice acts.
3. It can form the basis for a private tort action.

(See Chapter 10 for a discussion of EEOC suits and settlements.)

These private lawsuits follow the same process as other civil suits.

1. A complaint is filed.
2. The employer responds to the complaint.
3. The parties obtain relevant information about each other in a process called discovery.
4. During this time, mediation may be available in an effort to reach a settlement or the parties may be negotiating on their own informally.
5. If no settlement is reached, the case goes to trial.
6. The parties call their witnesses and provide their evidence.
7. The judge makes a ruling.
8. If the judge finds for the plaintiff, various remedies can be ordered.

TITLE VII CASE

In order to file a Title VII case in federal court, a plaintiff must obtain permission from the EEOC. (See Chapter 10 for an overview of the EEOC agency procedures.)

The EEOC will give its permission in one of two ways. First, after the EEOC process is completed and the case is closed, a victim of sexual harassment has ninety days after receiving a notice of a *right to sue* from the EEOC to file a lawsuit under Title VII. Second, a plaintiff can request a notice of *right to sue* from the EEOC one hundred eighty days after the charge was first filed with the Commission. In some courts, the plaintiff will be permitted to file a lawsuit within ninety days of receipt of the *right to sue* letter even if the EEOC has not finished its investigation. Some plaintiffs do this because of the backlog at the EEOC, which is estimated to have tens of thousands of cases awaiting resolution.

The first civil suits brought on behalf of sexual harassment victims were all quid pro quo cases, such as a supervisor demanding sexual favors of a worker he supervises as a condition of getting or keeping a job benefit. The plaintiff must prove that the sexual advances were unwelcome, and that it was because she rejected or submitted to the sexual advance or demand that some condition or term of her employment was affected.

The second—and by far the most common—type of civil suit for sexual harassment involves victims who are subjected to a hostile work environment. Typically, the scenario for this type of case is that a coworker or several coworkers engage in severe, sexually harassing conduct, and the conduct becomes pervasive, harmful, and causes the workplace to be intimidating, hostile, or offensive. As explained more thoroughly in Chapter 3, the plaintiff must show that the defendant's conduct was unwelcome in the workplace.

THE REASONABLE PERSON STANDARD

In whose eyes will a case be judged? Most courts use a *reasonable person standard*—what a reasonable or average person would do under the circumstances—to determine whether the plaintiff has established her case. The EEOC guidelines suggest that this standard "should consider the victim's perspective and not stereotyped notions of acceptable reasonable person standard behavior."

SEXUAL HISTORY OF THE PLAINTIFF

In an effort to show that conduct was welcomed, the employer may attempt to discover and use the sexual history of the plaintiff. Federal courts have frowned upon this. The *Federal Rules of*

Evidence govern what type of evidence is admissible in a lawsuit. The federal rules protect a plaintiff's privacy by protecting his or her sexual history. One court said "a person's private and consensual sexual activities do not constitute a waiver of his or her legal protections against unwanted and unsolicited sexual harassment."

Another court has noted the following.

> *Whether a sexual advance was welcome, or whether an alleged victim in fact perceived an environment to be sexually offensive, does not turn on the private sexual behavior of the alleged victim, because a woman's expectations about her work environment cannot be said to change depending upon her sexual sophistication. (Wallace v. Spucci, 217 F.3d 157 (2nd Cir. 2000).)*

Some states also provide protection, but many do not because their statutes only protect victims in criminal sexual assault cases, not civil sexual harassment cases. There are some exceptions, such as California, which only allows the sexual history of the victim with the offender.

PSYCHIATRIC EXAM

Courts have limited inquiry into the victim's mental state on the basis that simply because a plaintiff seeks recovery for sexual harassment does not mean that her thoughts are at issue. Ordinarily, an employer does not have a right to force the plaintiff to take a mental or psychiatric exam. However, if the plaintiff seeks damages for her mental injuries (in a claim of intentional infliction of emotional distress, for example) the employer defendant is entitled to get copies of the records from a psychiatrist, psychologist, or counselor.

REPEAT OFFENDERS

Some courts permit evidence to be introduced showing that the harasser had previously harassed other women in the workplace. This is important, because surveys show that many harassers are repeat offenders. This type of evidence is important to show that the harasser's purpose was not innocent and the conduct was not accidental. It establishes that the harasser has chosen to engage in the conduct on prior occasions or with similarly situated workers.

EMPLOYER DEFENSES

Once the plaintiff establishes the claim of sexual harassment, the employer is entitled to respond. In a quid pro quo case, for example, an employer may:

- disagree or
- explain that the worker was affected for a legitimate reason.

For example, the employer may explain that the decision to fire the worker was not based on gender, but instead was based on poor performance or absenteeism. In a hostile environment case, the employer may claim that it was isolated conduct or the conduct was not so severe that it affected the employee's work conditions, even if it was repeated.

In both types of cases, an employer can try to show that the conduct was welcomed by the plaintiff. In certain cases, the employer may also raise the defense that it had a sexual harassment policy but the victim failed to use it, so it never had a chance to remedy the situation.

PRETEXT

Once the employer puts on its case, the plaintiff is entitled to argue that the decisions made were *pretextual* (i.e., that it was a cover for the true motive of sexual harassment). For example, when the victim of harassment was the only person laid off, a court could find that the layoff was due to the harassment or in retaliation for reporting the harassment, despite the employer's argument that the layoff was because of a downturn in its business.

RETALIATION

Title VII forbids retaliating against a person who reports or cooperates in the investigation of a sexual harassment claim. A plaintiff is entitled to protection from retaliation for making the complaint, as is any worker who cooperated in the investigation of the complaint.

To determine whether subsequent action against a person who makes a claim of sexual harassment constitutes retaliation, the following questions are generally asked.

- Was the worker a person who filed a complaint of sexual harassment or did the worker cooperate in an investigation of such a complaint?
- Was the employer aware that the worker it took action against was part of the sexual harassment investigation?

- What negative action was the worker subjected to?
- Was that negative action caused by the pursuing of the complaint of sexual harassment?

In one case, a sergeant with the sheriff's department sexually harassed a court aid under his supervision. She said he forced her to have sex with him to get favorable treatment and avoid discipline in her job. The county settled her sexual harassment suit for $450,000. However, two months after she settled the lawsuit, the woman was fired. She sued for retaliation, because prior to being fired she was suspended several times—once she was even suspended for thirty days because she did not report for work on the day she gave pretrial testimony in the sexual harassment case. This employer did not learn its lesson the first time, and the county ended up agreeing to pay another $150,000 to settle the retaliation lawsuit.

In the case above, the sheriff's department knew the court aid was the plaintiff in the sexual harassment suit, and despite this fact, suspended her for pursuing her claim and actually fired her in retaliation. Therefore, it was a separate violation of her civil rights. This would be true even if she had not won her first case of sexual harassment. The law wants to encourage workers to pursue their civil rights, even if they cannot fully prove them. If employers were allowed to fire workers hoping they could not prove their claims, it would make it difficult for workers to take that risk and make the complaint.

REMEDIES

The remedies in a lawsuit depend on the type of suit filed. For example, a sexual harassment suit filed under Title VII or one of the state or local fair employment practice acts limits damages to certain types of employment losses. These remedies are designed to put the employee back in the position he or she was before the harassment occurred.

STATE FAIR EMPLOYMENT PRACTICE LAWS

Most states and some municipalities have passed fair employment practice laws that bar sexual harassment. These laws are similar to the federal law, but they have differences in coverage and remedies.

Reasons for pursuing a claim under the state or local law include:

- a longer period within which to file a claim;
- coverage of smaller employers;
- the ability to charge a supervisor personally; or,
- more favorable remedies.

For example, under New Jersey state law, the plaintiff has a much longer time within which to file (six years) than under federal law. Unlike federal law, California does not put a cap on damages, so the award might be larger. Also, some states, like Iowa and Washington, hold a supervisor personally responsible for his or her sexual harassment, but under federal law, it is the employer who is responsible. Finally, while federal law only applies only to employers with fifteen or more persons, some states cover smaller employers.

Your state agency can provide information on whether your city has a local ordinance prohibiting sexual harassment. To find your state's law and agency, see Appendix C.

SETTLING YOUR CASE

Some sexual harassment cases can be settled without the need
to go to an agency or file a lawsuit for help. A settlement usually has a much quicker resolution than a formal case, but a settlement means compromise. Rarely does either party get all they
feel is appropriate. Still, a settlement vindicates your claim and
may offer a resolution that everyone can live with. In evaluating
whether you should settle your sexual harassment complaint,
you should speak to an attorney, so you can weigh all your
options before deciding on a course of action.

The following are reasons to consider an informal settlement:
- the harassment is relatively minor;
- you want to continue working for the employer;
- you want to avoid the stress and publicity of a more
  formal claim;
- you are ready to put the event behind you and move
  forward;
- you recognize that settlement means compromise; or,
- you seek to have the greatest flexibility in agreeing to
  terms.

An informal settlement works best when the harassment is relatively minor and the parties desire to continue to work together.
If the sexual harassment is an isolated event and not widespread
throughout the company, individual solutions are more easily
reached. However, pervasive sexual harassment is rarely
resolved on a case-by-case basis. The harassment itself should
not involve physical contact that raises a safety issue, because
an informal settlement is unlikely to resolve such a serious risk
to your safety.

There is increased stress when a claim moves into a formal process. Along with an increase in stress is the greater publicity that a formal claim can attract. Publicity can be a good thing, because it helps draw focus and attention to intolerable work situations, and sometimes helps to put pressure on an employer to resolve a case. Publicity may also mean that parties become entrenched in their positions and refuse to work towards a settlement.

Considerations in Settling Your Case

Just as you have suffered losses as the victim of sexual harassment, your claim will cost the employer considerable costs in attorney fees, productivity, reputation, and morale. To save these considerable costs, both parties may wish to think about settling the case.

To consider what you want to settle a case for, make a list of all of your losses (financial, emotional, and psychological) since the sexual harassment began. Consider the following:

- lost wages;
- sick, vacation, or personal time used;
- sick, vacation, or other time you would have accumulated during any time off;
- medical or counseling bills;
- cost of reinstatement of other benefits you would have accrued (such as pension or profit sharing lost); and,
- legal costs incurred.

Once you have made your list, consider other items that are important to you, such as:

- what conditions you need to feel safe in the workplace if the harasser has not been fired or transferred and

- what kind of statement the company will make concerning your complaint. (In other words, should there
  be a statement in the company newsletter or in the
  monthly email?)

There are additional things to consider if you do not intend to
return to work. These can be more complex to calculate and
often will require additional expertise from an attorney. The
agreement should include:

- that the employer will provide a positive reference,
  both orally and in writing (have an example letter to
  attach to the agreement);
- that you might benefit from counseling;
- that the employer agrees to pay for job placement
  services; and,
- consideration of the loss of future wages and benefits,
  such as pension benefits.

Settlement agreements may be short or long, but what is most
important is that they address your particular circumstances. A
settlement can be a very good way to obtain resolution of your
claim, but be aware of what you are signing. For example, the
employer's attorney often drafts the agreement, and may include
language that settles "all claims you have and may have against"
your employer. However, that language may later be construed
to include an act of retaliation or a personal injury claim that
you did not realize you signed away at the settlement. The
employer may also want to include a confidentiality clause that
affects what you can and cannot say about the harassment and
the terms of the settlement. Further, a settlement agreement may
have tax consequences to you. For all these reasons, it is critical

that before you sign any agreement to settle your case, you seek competent legal advice.

TORT ACTION

In some instances, a plaintiff who files suit under the antidiscrimination laws can also add private claims, which might provide additional remedies. Sometimes, plaintiffs will not file under antidiscrimination laws at all. In such a case, there is no requirement that any claims be first filed with an antidiscrimination agency, like the EEOC. Instead, the plaintiff can go directly to court. These decisions are best made after consulting with an attorney. See Chapter 14 for more information on finding an attorney.

Torts are lawsuits that claim a wrongful act injured another, and for which the law imposes civil liability. Common claims in these lawsuits include assault and battery, defamation, false imprisonment, invasion of privacy, or outrage (also known as the intentional infliction of emotional distress).

Assault & Battery

These actions are often brought together, but they are two distinct theories. An *assault* involves a threat of harm, while a *battery* involves the actual harmful or offensive contact. This tort occurs when, for example, a supervisor or coworker threatens harm or actually pushes or grabs the plaintiff. The damages recoverable do not have a maximum cap.

Defamation

The basis for this suit occurs when a person makes false statements to others that injure the plaintiff's reputation. The statement can be made verbally or in writing. In one case, after the female worker rejected the sexual advances of her supervisor, he told other employees that she was a lesbian. In most cases, the plaintiff will have to prove that the statement harmed his or her reputation either by examining the nature of the statement itself or by showing how the plaintiff's reputation suffered as a result. Like the other torts, the damages recoverable do not have a maximum cap.

False Imprisonment

If the victim has been pinned against the wall or picked up, she might include a claim of *false imprisonment*, which requires her to show that she was held in a location against her will by a person without authority to do so. The damages recoverable are not subject to a cap.

Invasion of Privacy

Persons have right to privacy, and intrusion on the privacy of another may result in a claim of *invasion of privacy*. Usually, this results in a claim that there was public disclosure of private facts or an unreasonable intrusion into the plaintiff's private life. This tort does not have a maximum cap for damages, but the plaintiff must show the harm that occurred as a result of the invasion of privacy.

Outrage or Intentional Infliction of Emotional Distress

When the conduct of the defendant is intentional and outrageous, and causes the plaintiff harm or severe emotional suffering, it can form the basis of a suit for *intentional infliction of emotional distress*. Sometimes this claim is called *outrage*. This tort is frequently joined to sexual harassment complaints. Like the other torts, damages recoverable do not have a cap. However, the facts must *shock the conscience* or be otherwise outrageous to recover under this theory.

CRIMINAL OFFENSES

The conduct, which underlies sexual harassment, may extend to criminal liability for the person who commits the assault or battery. Harassing a person by telephone may be criminally charged as telephone harassment under certain circumstances. Sexual crimes may be charged for the touching, fondling, and more severe sexual conduct cases. Each state's laws differ, but violence should always be reported to the police.

THE HARASSER CAN SUE

Harassers can sue. Most who do, sue their employer for improper discharge. However, generally courts are not sympathetic to their claims, and find that the employer had a valid reason for the discharge.

In one well-known case, a worker discussed with a coworker an episode of the television show *Seinfeld*, in which Jerry Seinfeld could not remember the name of a woman he was dating, except that the woman's name rhymed with a part of the female body.

He asked his coworker to guess which one it was. He even copied a page of a dictionary with the term. The coworker, embarrassed by the discussion, made a formal complaint of sexual harassment that resulted in the firing of the jokester. The terminated *harasser* sued and won a $26 million dollar judgment, including a $1.5 million dollar judgment against the woman who complained. Both judgments were overturned on appeal. It turns out that the terminated worker had been warned about using sexually explicit language in the past, and the company even had to pay out a prior judgment due to his conduct.

At times, the employer does not follow its own policies and can be held liable to an employee it fired for sexual harassment. For example, an employer who fired a worker for sexual harassment was ordered to pay $40,000 in lost wages when it violated its own disciplinary policies. The employer was also ordered to pay the harasser's attorney's fees. (*Jesso v. Letica Corp.*, 2000 Mich. App. LEXIS 2812 (Mi. App. 2000).)

Section Four:
Legal Resources

chapter twelve:
Legal Research

Laws can be found in statutes or codes of both the federal and state government. The federal and state laws are found in the codes that are listed in Appendices B and C, respectively. To find your laws, you will need to do some basic legal research.

STATUTES OR CODES

A large public library may carry some legal books, but a specialized law library will have the most up-to-date version of the governmental codes, as well as other types of research materials not found in a regular public library. Law libraries can usually be found at or near the local courthouse—your court clerk's office should be able to tell you where to find the law library. Also, any law school will have a law library.

Contact the closest law library to determine hours and directions. Ask if there are any restrictions on the use of the library by members of the general public. Some law libraries may have limitations (such as limited hours or days) for non-attorneys. Law school libraries may have similar (or stricter) restrictions for nonstudents.

Your first step will probably be to find the basic law in the federal and state statutes or codes. The actual title of the set of books containing the statutes or codes is very important. Refer to the listings in Appendix C to find the title of the appropriate books. Reference librarians can help you find the set of books you are looking for. Once you find the proper set of books, look for the section, title, or other numbers listed in Appendix C in order to find the exact provisions of the laws.

For example, if you are looking at the listing in Appendix B for the Title VII of the United States Civil Rights Act (which is the federal statute that prohibits sexual harassment in employment) after the heading "The Law," you will see the notation 42 U.S.C. §2000e. This gives you the Title (42) and Section (2000e) of the set of books (*United States Code*).

NOTE: *The U.S. Code also comes in two annotated versions called the* **United States Code Service** *(U.S.C.S.), and the* **United States Code Annotated** *(U.S.C.A.). The U.S.C.S. and U.S.C.A. versions of the statutes contain helpful notes and references to make them easier to use.*

As you continue to look at the appendix information for the federal statute, you will also see the notation "2000e" under the heading "Scope." This tells you that the portion of the law relating to who is a covered employer for purposes of the Civil Rights Act is found at Section 2000e of Title 42 of the United States Code. The legal citation for this section would be 42 U.S.C. §2000e.

Similarly, if you look at the listing for Illinois in Appendix C, you will see the notation "West's Illinois Compiled Statutes Annotated, Chapter 775, Article 5, Section 1-101 (775 ILCS 5/1-

101)" after the heading "The Law." This gives you the Title (775) and Section (5/1-101) of the set of books (*West's Illinois Compiled Statutes Annotated*). You will also note the notation "5/2-101" under the heading "Scope." The Illinois Human Rights Act is found at Chapter 775 of the Illinois Compiled Statutes in Article 5 at Section 2-101. The legal citation for this section would be 775 ILCS 5/2-101.

Once you locate the specific laws, check to see if there is a more current version available. This may be in the form of an update in the back of the volume, a separate update volume, or in some other format. If necessary, ask a reference librarian for assistance in order to be certain you have the most recent version. The statutes may also be annotated with short summaries of court decisions that have interpreted the statutes.

CASE REPORTERS

There are federal case decisions that have interpreted the federal sexual harassment statutes. Your state courts may also have interpreted your state's laws. If you wish to find the court's entire opinion, it will be included in the federal, state, or regional case reporter.

The federal case reporters contain court opinions from the federal courts. Cases from the United States Supreme Court appear in *United States Reports* (U.S.), in the *Supreme Court Reports* (S. Ct.), or in the *Lawyers' Edition* (L. Ed.). Cases from the federal courts of appeal appear in the *Federal Reports* (F.), which has a second (F.2d) and is currently in the third series (F.3d). Cases from the federal trial courts appear in the *Federal Supplement Reporters* (F. Supp.).

A state case reporter, such as the *Illinois Reports*, contains court opinions from the courts of a single state. A regional reporter, such as the *North Eastern Reports*, contains cases from the courts of several states in a certain geographic area.

To find a case, carefully copy down the case name and the numbers that follow it (called the *citation*), or make a copy of the page with the case information. Next, locate the *case reporters* in the library. Ask your reference librarian for assistance.

The United States Supreme Court's cases may be found in either the United States Reports or in the Supreme Court Reports, as follows.

NAME OF CASE	UNITED STATES REPORTER	PARALLEL REPORTER	YEAR PUBLISHED

Once you find the proper federal reporter, the citation is found using the following method.

524	U.S.	742
Volume	*Reporter*	*Page Number*

On page 742 of Volume 524 of the United States Reports case reporter, you should find the Supreme Court's opinion in *Burlington Industries, Inc. v. Ellerth*, which was decided in 1998.

Many states have more than one reporter in which the same case can be found. The stated citation often looks like the following.

NAME OF CASE	STATE CASE REPORTER	REGIONAL REPORTER	YEAR PUBLISHED

Once you find the proper state or regional reporter, the citation is found using the similar method as detailed on the previous page.

178	Ill.App.	3d	1033
Volume	*State Court*	*Series Version*	*Page Number*

Thus, on page 1033 of Volume 178 of Illinois Appellate 3d series case reporter, you should find the appellate court opinion in *State v. Human Rights Comm'n*, decided in 1989 by the fourth district appellate court. After a point, instead of continuing to increase the volume numbers, publishers started over with volume one of a subsequent series of the reporter. In our example, you would actually find three series of books on the library shelves: one titled Illinois Appellate Reports; another titled Illinois Appellate Reports, Second Series (2d); and, a third titled Illinois Appellate Reports, Third Series (3d). Each set begins with Volume I. The Third Series contains the most recent cases. Check to see if the law has been updated or revised by checking for a pocket part or supplement.

INTERNET RESEARCH

Increasingly, the Internet is becoming a resource to obtain legal information. The federal government and many states include their statutes and selected cases on their government websites. For example, the Equal Employment Opportunity Commission maintains a website at **www.eeoc.gov**. These sites typically contain helpful information and explanations about sexual harassment.

Searching the Internet is based on URLs (Uniform Resource Locators), also known as *Web addresses*, or by using key words in a search engine. An easy way to find legal information is by typing your question or some key words into a search engine, such as *Yahoo!* or *Google*. Another easy way to find available Web information on laws is by searching the *lawcrawler* search engine by FindLaw. Type in **www.findlaw.com**, then choose either federal or state cases and codes to search for the appropriate information.

Researching on the Internet can be much faster than looking up the federal or state laws in the books, but online research produces only a screen snapshot at a time, so you may need to open several pages to see the whole set of laws you are seeking. When working online, be sure to review all of the relevant website information, then download or print the portion of the law in which you are interested.

LEGAL ENCYCLOPEDIAS

You should also be able to find sets of books called *legal encyclopedias* at a law library. These are similar to a regular encyclopedia, in that you look up the subject (such as sexual harassment) and it gives you a summary of the law on that subject, along with citations to court cases that relate to that subject. There are two national legal encyclopedias. One is *American Jurisprudence* (Am. Jur.) and the other is *Corpus Juris Secundum* (C.J.S.). Many states have their own legal encyclopedias, such as *Florida Jurisprudence* (Fla. Jur.) and *Texas Jurisprudence* (Tex. Jur.). Like the case reporters, these may also have multiple series.

DIGESTS

Another type of book found in law libraries is called a *digest*. Like a legal encyclopedia, you look up the subject, but instead of giving you a summary of the law, it gives you summaries of court cases discussing that subject of the law. A national digest exists, published by West Publishing called the *Decennial Digest* (it is grouped in ten-year increments). For state law, search for a digest specific to your state. Again, there may be multiple series.

FORM AND PRACTICE GUIDES

All law libraries have certain form and practice manuals that include the laws, procedures, and forms used in the federal or state jurisdiction. These can be most helpful in preparing forms or finding forms. Never hesitate to ask a reference librarian for assistance in finding a practice guide in the law library.

chapter thirteen:
Mediation and Arbitration

Mediation and arbitration are two methods of resolving a sexual harassment claim without going through the more formal court process of a lawsuit. These methods are sometimes called *alternative dispute resolution*, and are becoming more common as employers seek ways to save on the high cost of legal claims. Mediation tends to work best when both parties want to try to resolve the problem and continue a working relationship. Arbitration, while cheaper than a lawsuit, may tend to favor an employer, and should be carefully scrutinized by an employee before being considered as a method of a resolving sexual harassment claim.

MEDIATION

Mediation is a form of alternative dispute resolution (ADR). This type of legal remedy may be available pursuant to employer policy. It is also offered by the EEOC as an alternative to the traditional lawsuit. After a charge is filed, mediation will be offered in appropriate cases. *Mediation* is an informal process in which a neutral third party assists the opposing parties to reach a voluntary, negotiated resolution.

The decision to mediate is completely voluntary for both parties. Mediation has many benefits. It gives the parties the opportunity to discuss the issues raised in the charge and come to an agreement. A trained mediator does not force the parties to agree, but helps them work out an agreement that both parties can live with. The mediation process is usually governed by confidentiality requirements. For example, in EEOC mediation, information disclosed during mediation will not be revealed to anyone, including other EEOC employees. If mediation is not successful, the victim of harassment can continue to pursue the charge filed with the appropriate agency. A mediation agreement is subject to enforcement just like a court settlement or judgment.

Advantages of Mediation

One of the biggest advantages of mediation is that unlike a private lawsuit, agency mediation is generally free. In this way it saves time and money. According to the EEOC, many mediations are completed in a single session. A party can have an attorney present, but is not required to do so. Parties to a mediation should be required to sign a confidentiality agreement so that all of the discussion remains confidential. An independent survey of EEOC cases in mediation showed 96% of all defendants and 91% of all plaintiffs who used mediation would use it again if offered. In EEOC cases in 2003, the mediation program achieved a 69% settlement rate. Most settled cases include monetary and nonmonetary benefits.

Mediation Strategies

Research has examined what qualities contribute to resolving cases of sexual harassment in mediation. For individuals who have filed a complaint, honesty and openness to a realistic, good faith resolution are critical to settling a case. These parties are also focused and come prepared. They know what they want and they stay focused and prepared. This does not mean they are rigid, though. They know their facts, and they do not let the fact that their employer brings an attorney to the session intimidate them. Some of these parties also have their own lawyer, and are willing to seek closure and carefully follow their attorney's advice in resolving the case. One behavior that interferes with the settlement process is anger. The need to blame and vent is not a positive mediation strategy for charging parties.

The same flexibility and openness was required of employers to succeed in resolving a case in mediation. These employers had a good faith willingness to negotiate or to explore settlement options. For example, in one study of EEOC cases, nearly 15% were resolved in mediation when the employer provided an apology, admitted the sexual harassment, or at least recognized the concerns of the victim of harassment. Simply listening to the victim of harassment contributed to resolving the case about 10% of the time. Indeed, these employers came to the mediation with a commitment to resolve the complaint. Employers who were considered arrogant or unrealistically harsh were seen as obstacles to the mediation process.

The goal of mediation is to find a resolution if possible, and one of the most important strategies of both parties was to recognize the other's position and expression of needs. For employers, acknowledgement of the harm done to the victim of harassment was important. An admission of some liability may reduce the need to place blame and allow the parties to move forward in settlement.

For additional information on mediation, contact your EEOC office or state fair employment agency. Addresses are listed in Appendix A.

ARBITRATION

Unlike mediation, arbitration is a tool used by employers to limit or eliminate certain procedural obligations under the law. Although the United States Supreme Court has permitted employers to use arbitration agreements (*Gilmer v. Interstate/Johnson Lane Corp.*, 500 U.S. 33 (1991)), the EEOC has said that agreements that mandate arbitration of sexual harassment complaints are intrinsically unfair.[21]

Some employers require that applicants and employees give up their right to pursue employment discrimination claims in court and agree to resolve disputes through binding arbitration as a condition of employment. Arbitration clauses are sometimes included in employee agreements or handbooks. They may delete certain remedies otherwise available to the employee. They may also require fees to be paid by the employee who is filing a complaint.

If you are asked to sign an arbitration clause, make sure that at a minimum, the procedures provide that arbitration will be conducted by an independent and impartial arbitrator chosen by agreement of both parties. Also, the arbitrator should have the same power to award any remedy available under law. Both parties should have equal access to discovery and witnesses, and employees must have the right to be represented by an attorney.

chapter fourteen:
The Role of Lawyers

Cases involving sexual harassment are considered civil cases, as opposed to criminal ones. A victim of sexual harassment will have to get and pay for a lawyer herself. In some cases, though, there are legal aid clinics and law school programs that can provide free or low-cost legal assistance.

It is up to you to decide if you want or need a lawyer, but before you decide to make any major changes in your workplace, talk to a lawyer. If you decide to file a complaint with a federal or state agency, or decide that a private lawsuit is necessary, you should at least consult with a lawyer to consider all of your options.

As you are evaluating your options with a lawyer, the lawyer is likely evaluating your case. Lawyers decide whether to take cases based on a number of factors, including cost, time, effort, and the potential for collection of fees.

LAWYERS AND CONFIDENTIALITY

To encourage people to speak freely to their lawyers, the law provides confidentiality protection for clients. This is called the *attorney/client privilege*. The privilege prevents a lawyer from disclosing your information under most circumstances. Be honest in disclosing all the facts surrounding your employment, even those facts which are embarrassing or humiliating. The lawyer will need this information to properly evaluate the case.

FINDING A LAWYER

The search for a lawyer can take some time and no small amount of perseverance. Just as people specialize in other professions, it is becoming rare today to find a lawyer that has a general practice. The lawyer you choose should have experience in cases similar to yours.

Recommendations from Friends

A lawyer is often contacted based on the strength of recommendations by family or friends. These recommendations can be helpful, because the good experience of your family member or friend may provide reliable information on the quality of service provided by the lawyer.

Referral Services

If you do not personally know a lawyer and do not have a recommendation from a trusted friend or family member, you can look to other sources. In most cities there is a local bar association, which is an organization that many local attorneys will belong to. The bar association can help make lawyer referrals, either formally or informally. Sometimes lawyers may list their practice in the Yellow Pages of the phone book under "Lawyer" or "Attorney." Some may advertise, or you may read about a lawyer's representation of another sexual harassment case in the paper or see something about it on television.

Prepaid Legal Plans

If you are covered by a prepaid legal plan, check to see whether a consultation for an employment-related issue is covered.

Website

Another area to search for finding a lawyer is on the Internet. Some lawyers now have websites and list their services and contact information. Even if you do not have access to the Internet at home, most public libraries now have Internet computers for use by library patrons.

Legal Clinics

In larger populations, there are often legal clinics that provide low-cost legal representation in employment matters. Some low-income individuals may also qualify for free legal representation.

Law Schools

Some law schools maintain clinical programs that take cases. Be sure to check with any area law schools to see if any programs exist and whether your case would be eligible for service. If the clinic does accept your case, you might not be required to pay or you might pay on a sliding fee scale.

Attorney Registration

Every state maintains a registration of lawyers who practice law within that state. To find the phone number and address of any lawyer within your state, contact the bar association or other attorney registration office within your state. To find your local bar association, simply look in the Yellow Pages under "lawyer referrals."

INITIAL CONTACT

The selection of a lawyer usually begins with a phone call. In this first contact with the lawyer, be sure to obtain some preliminary information and write it down. Make sure to get answers to the following questions.

- Does this lawyer charge for a consultation?
- How long will the first meeting be?
- How much does the lawyer usually charge for his or her services?

Compare the answers given by the lawyers you speak to, then decide which ones to meet with for an initial consultation.

FIRST INTERVIEW

The first interview with a lawyer is very important. Remember that you have not agreed to anything other than the terms of the initial visit. Do not be intimidated by the thought of meeting with the lawyer. You are under no obligation to sign or agree to anything at this time, and you can take any written documents home to think about before you sign. Also, be sure to write down any information you obtain from the lawyers you speak to. It will help you remember who said what later.

Follow your instincts and trust your evaluation of the lawyer when you meet. Do you like this lawyer? Do you feel that he or she is listening to you and your situation? Are you treated with respect during your visit by the office staff? Your intuition will tell you a great deal about whether you should proceed further with this lawyer.

In telling the lawyer about your case, be as clear and concise as possible. You will want to bring relevant documents that will help the lawyer to understand the facts of your case. Discuss what the lawyer thinks the projected costs will be and how you will be billed for those costs.

FEE ARRANGEMENTS

In some types of discrimination cases, attorneys charge hourly fees in addition to the expenses of the case. Most attorneys are expensive, charging more than $100 per hour, and may require a substantial initial payment (a *retainer*) from you to begin the case. (Remember, a court may order the wrongdoer to pay for your attorney's fees if you win.)

If a retainer is to be paid, make sure that you and your lawyer agree what minimum services are to be provided for that sum. For example, for a retainer of $500 or more, the lawyer should at least prepare and file your complaint, and have the employer or defendant served. What you want to avoid is a situation where you pay your lawyer a retainer, he or she writes a letter and makes a few phone calls to the other side's attorney, then tells you the retainer is used up and more money is required to continue your case.

In sexual harassment cases that are brought under the federal statutes and some state's statutes, attorney's fees can be ordered paid by the employer if you are successful in your case. It may also be possible to have certain costs—such as out-of-pocket expenses, postage, faxes, copies, long-distance calls, and travel for your attorney, paralegals, and even expert witness fees—be ordered paid by the other side.

In some private lawsuits, lawyers will usually take the case on a percentage of the potential judgment (usually one-third, but can be up to 40%). If there is no judgment, then no fees will be due.

NOTE: *You will still be responsible to pay for the expenses of filing the documents, photocopying, telephone charges, postage, transcript, reporter, and service-type fees.*

However your fee is arranged, make sure that you have it in writing so there will be no confusion as to what is owed, and when and how it should be paid.

WORKING WITH THE LAWYER

Once you decide to hire the lawyer and he or she agrees to take the case, be sure to let the lawyer know what kind of client you are. How involved do you want to be in the case? Do you want to be informed of each step in the case? Would you like copies of each document the lawyer files or receives in your case? (Realize that you may be expected to pay for copies.) Alternatively, you may ask you lawyer to make the file available to you on a regular basis to view at his or her office to keep current with developments in your case.

Your lawyer should be able to take you through the case step-by-step to explain the procedures and anticipated timeline in your case. Ask the lawyer how often you can expect him or her to notify you about your case. If you know the general timeline of your case, it will help you understand how often to expect contact from the lawyer. For example, depending on the theory of your case, your lawyer may file a complaint with the federal or state fair employment agency before commencing a lawsuit in court. Once your *right to sue* letter is received, your complaint is then able to be filed with the court. This process can take several months. Set up a method of contact that is convenient for you and reasonable for your lawyer.

Endnotes

1. C. Safran, "What Men Do To Women On the Job," Redbook Magazine (Nov. 1976) (reader questionnaire).
2. R. Sandroff, "Sexual Harassment: The Inside Story," Working Woman, p.47 (June 1992).
3. U.S. Merit Systems Protection Board, Sexual Harassment of Federal Workers: Is it a Problem? Washington, D.C.: U.S. Gov't Printing Office (1981); U.S. Merit Systems Protection Board, Sexual Harassment of Federal Workers: An Update. Washington, D.C.: U.S.Gov't Printing Office (1987); and. U.S. Merit Systems Protection Board, Sexual Harassment in the Federal Workplace: Trends, Progress, Continuing Challenges. Washington, D.C.: U.S. Gov't Printing Office (1994).
4. Klein Assoc., Inc., The 1988 Working Women Sexual Harassment Survey Executive Report, Klein Associates, Inc. Cambridge, MA (1988).
5. A. Bryant, "Hostile Hallways: The AAUW Survey On Sexual Harassment in America's Schools," J. of School Health, No. 63, pages 355–357 (1993) (reporting statistics on the AAUW survey).
6. G. Gipson, "Two Wins for Working Women," Baltimore Sun, Journal Gazette, Indiana (July 19, 2004).

7. "Sexual Harassment: It's About Power, Not Lust," New York Times (Oct. 22, 1991).

8. C. White, B. Angle, and M. Moore, "Sexual Harassment in the Coal Industry: A Survey of Women Miners," Oak Ridge, Tennessee: Coal Employment Project (1981).

9. E. Lafontaine and L. Treadeau, "The Frequency, Sources, and Correlates of Sexual Harassment among Women in Traditional Male Occupations," Sex Roles, pages 433–442 (1986).

10. National Center for Women & Policing, "Equality Denied: The Status of Women and Policing 2001," (April, 2002).

11. "LAPD Settles ACLU Sexual Assault Case for $165,000; Case Symbolizes Persistent Sexual Harassment, Gender Inequities," (ACLU press release, Jan. 25, 1995) available at: **www.aclu.org**.

12. Chris Fleszar, "Female Grand Rapids Police Officers Awarded $2.5 Million by Jury." (Although the officers originally lost their case, two appealed and a jury awarded them $2.5 million.)

13. Santa Cruz Sentinel, June 15, 2004.

14. Eric Schmitt, "The Military Has a Lot To Learn About Women," The New York Times Book Review (Aug. 2, 1992).

15. N. Korecki, "Ex-Hooters Girl Wins $275,000 in Sexual Harassment Lawsuit," Sun-Times (Nov. 24, 2004).

16. J.G. Keil, "Wall Streeter Wants Back In," New York Post (April 10, 2005).

17. Comments of Radika Coomaraswamy, United Nations Special Rapporteur on Violence Against Women (1994–2003) as reported in 1997 Report of the Special Rapporteur on Violence Against Women, UN Commission on Human Rights.

18. Peggy Crull, "The Stress Effects of Sexual Harassment on the Job," Academic and Workplace Sexual Harassment: A Resource Manual (Michele A. Paludi and Richard B. Barickman) (NY Press, 1991).

19. Orlando Sentinel (July 20, 1993) and NAT'L L.J. (May 30, 1994).
20. U.S. Merit Systems Protection Board Studies, supra note #3.
21. EEOC Policy Statement on Mandatory Binding Arbitration of Employment Discrimination Disputes as a Condition of Employment, July 10, 1997.

Glossary

A

assault. To threaten another with force or use of force. An assault is both a crime and a civil wrong, so the victim who is assaulted can sue for damages.

assault and battery. Often in a civil complaint, an assault (threat) is joined with the actual harm threatened (battery).

attorney/client privilege. The legal right of an attorney to keep nearly all client information confidential.

B

back pay. The payment of past wages or benefits lost due to sexual harassment.

battery. An intentional or unlawful touching of a victim. Like the tort of assault, a battery is both a crime and a civil wrong, so the victim can sue for damages.

C

civil lawsuit. A lawsuit filed as a result of a violation of a civil right (such as sexual harassment), created by common law or statute.

complainant. The person who files the complaint.

complaint. The pleading document by which a civil lawsuit begins.

corroborate. To supplement, or add to, the testimony or information of another person or evidence.

D

damages. The money portion of remedies available to compensate the losses of the sexual harassment victim. Damages can be ordered by a court or agreed upon through a settlement. *See also remedies and punitive damages.*

defamation. A claim in a civil lawsuit that is based on the harm to one's reputation. Slander is the spoken form of defamation, while libel is written.

defendant. A person, employee, or other party who is sued.

E

Equal Employment Opportunity Commission (EEOC). The agency charged with enforcing laws against sexual harassment in the workplace.

EEOC guidelines. The interpretation of the Civil Rights laws that the EEOC will use to enforce the sexual harassment laws.

employee. A person who is hired to perform work for another person, company, or school.

employer. A person or company who hires a person to perform work.

evidence. Proof that supports a party's case.

F

Fair Employment Protection Agency (FEPA). A state's fair employment agency.

front pay. The payment of future wages or benefits lost due to sexual harassment.

G

general civility code. A set of social rules in which people treat others with respect.

H

hostile work environment. A type of sexual harassment claim in which the plaintiff cannot demonstrate that she was fired, but the environment has so much harassing conduct that it will still be considered sexual harassment. Also called *hostile environment*.

I

injunction. A court order that either prohibits or compels the performance of a particular action. For example, a court may order a company to develop a sexual harassment policy or hold training. An injunction can also order a company to cease any sexually harassing activity.

intentional infliction of emotional distress. A type of claim in a civil lawsuit stating that an employee suffered emotional distress from an employer's outrageous conduct. This claim is sometimes called the tort of *outrage*.

L

love contract. Not really a contract at all, but a method used by employers to avoid responsibility for addressing sexual harassment.

M

mediation. A process by which a claim can be resolved without going to trial.

mitigation of damages. The duty of a sexual harassment victim to reduce loss. For example, if a person loses her job due to sexual harassment, she has a duty to use reasonable efforts to seek other comparable employment.

P

pain and suffering. A part of a claim for money damages that is based on the plaintiff's mental and emotional distress.

plaintiff. A person who files a civil lawsuit.

punitive damages. The money awarded to punish a company or other sexual harasser that has engaged in willful or malicious conduct. In some jurisdictions, this is also called *exemplary damages*.

Q

quid pro quo. A Latin phrase that means "something for something." It is one of the types of sexual harassment claims in which a supervisor, for example, conditions a raise on submission to sex.

R

reasonable person standard. The measure by which a person's actions will be judged as reasonable. The reasonable person will be presumed to exercise due care and ordinary judgment in responding to a situation. In this way, the law can establish a basis by which to measure the reasonableness of conduct.

remedies. The methods by which a person who is victimized by sexual harassment can recover her or his losses. The law permits back pay, reinstatement, future earnings, and money damages due to pain and suffering in sexual harassment cases.

retaliation. Acts of a company designed to get revenge for a complaint of sexual harassment or to punish an employee for cooperating in an investigation of sexual harassment.

right-to-sue letter. The letter issued by the EEOC that gives a worker permission to file a discrimination lawsuit against an employer in federal court.

S

sex discrimination. The illegal and unfair treatment of an employee because of that employee's sex.

sexual harassment. Unwanted sexual conduct or words in the workplace that can be the basis of a civil rights complaint. The two types are *quid pro quo* and *hostile work environment*.

sexual harassment policy. The process and procedures a company uses to make decisions about how it will respond to sexual harassment.

sexual stereotyping. Judging a person with preconceived notions of gender. For example, the view that women are not tough enough to be police officers.

strict liability. A policy that imposes responsibility on an employer for sexual harassment because the harasser is a supervisor.

T

Title VII. The portion of the Civil Rights Act of federal law that prohibits sexual harassment in the workplace by employers with fifteen or more employees.

tort. A private or civil wrong that causes injury to a person.

U

unwelcome conduct. Behavior or conduct that is not consented to by the person it is targeted at. This must be shown in sexual harassment cases (except where the victim is a minor).

appendix a:
U.S. Equal Employment Opportunity Commission Offices

In 2005, the Equal Employment Opportunity Commission Offices began planning a restructuring of certain offices. Check for current information about the EEOC and the laws it enforces at **www.eeoc.gov**.

HEADQUARTERS

U.S. Equal Employment Opportunity Commission
    1801 L Street, NW
    Washington, DC 20507
    202-663-4900
    TTY: 202-663-4494

FIELD OFFICES

To be automatically connected with the nearest EEOC field office, call:
    800-669-4000
    TTY: 800-669-6820

Albuquerque Area Office
505 Marquette Street, NW
Suite 900
Albuquerque, NM 87102
505-248-5201
TTY: 505-248-5240

Atlanta District Office
Sam Nunn Atlanta Federal Center
100 Alabama Street, SW
Suite 4R30
Atlanta, GA 30303
404-562-6800
TTY: 404-562-6801

Baltimore District Office
City Crescent Building
10 South Howard Street
Third Floor
Baltimore, MD 21201
410-962-3932
TTY: 410-962-6065

Birmingham District Office
Ridge Park Place
1130 22nd Street
Suite 2000
Birmingham, AL 35205
205-212-2100
TTY: 205-212-2112

Boston Area Office
   John F. Kennedy Federal Building
   475 Government Center
   Boston, MA 02203
   617-565-3200
   TTY: 617-565-3204

Buffalo Local Office
   6 Fountain Plaza
   Suite 350
   Buffalo, NY 14202
   716-551-4441
   TTY: 716-551-5923

Charlotte District Office
   129 West Trade Street
   Suite 400
   Charlotte, NC 28202
   704-344-6682
   704-344-6684

Chicago District Office
   500 West Madison Street
   Suite 2800
   Chicago, IL 60661
   312-353-2713
   TTY: 312-353-2421

Cincinnati Area Office
　　John W. Peck Federal Office Building
　　550 Main Street
　　Tenth Floor
　　Cincinnati, OH 45202
　　513-684-2851
　　TTY: 513-684-2074

Cleveland District Office
　　Tower City
　　Skylight Office Tower
　　1660 West Second Street
　　Suite 850
　　Cleveland, OH 44113-1412
　　216-522-2003
　　TTY: 216-522-8441

Dallas District Office
　　207 South Houston Street
　　Third Floor
　　Dallas, TX 75202
　　214-253-2700
　　TTY: 214-253-2710

Denver District Office
　　303 East 17th Avenue
　　Suite 510
　　Denver, CO 80203
　　303-866-1300
　　TTY: 303-866-1950

Detroit District Office
   Patrick V. McNamara Building
   477 Michigan Avenue
   Room 865
   Detroit, MI 48226-9704
   313-226-4600
   TTY: 313-226-7599

El Paso Area Office
   300 East Main Drive
   Suite 500
   El Paso, TX 79901
   915-534-6700
   TTY: 915-534-6710

Fresno Local Office
   1265 West Shaw Avenue
   Suite 103
   Fresno, CA 93711
   559-487-5793
   TTY: 559-487-5837

Greensboro Local Office
   2303 West Meadowview Road
   Suite 201
   Greensboro, NC 27407
   336-547-4188
   TTY: 336-547-4035

Greenville Local Office
301 North Main Street
Suite 1402
Greenville, SC 29601-9916
864-241-4400
TTY: 864-241-4403

Honolulu Local Office
300 Ala Moana Boulevard
Room 7-127
P.O. Box 50082
Honolulu, HI 96850-0051
808-541-3120
TTY: 808-541-3131

Houston District Office
Mickey Leland Federal Building
1919 Smith Street
Suites 600 and 700
Houston, TX 77002
713-209-3320
TTY: 713-209-3439

Indianapolis District Office
101 West Ohio Street
Suite 1900
Indiana, IN 46204
317-226-7212
TTY: 317-226-5162

Jackson Area Office
Dr. A.H. McCoy Federal Building
100 West Capitol Street
Suite 207
Jackson, MS 39269
601-965-4537
TTY: 601-965-4915

Kansas City Area Office
Gateway Tower II
Fourth and State Avenue
Ninth Floor
Kansas City, KS 66101
913-551-5655
TTY: 913-551-5657

Little Rock Area Office
820 Louisiana Street
Suite 200
Little Rock, AR 72201
501-324-5060
TTY: 501-324-5481

Los Angeles District Office
Roybal Federal Building
255 East Temple
Fourth Floor
Los Angeles, CA 90012
213-894-1000
TTY: 213-894-1121

Louisville Area Office
   600 Dr. Martin Luther King, Jr. Place
   Suite 268
   Louisville, KY 40202
   502-582-6082
   TTY: 502-582-6285

Memphis District Office
   1407 Union Avenue
   Suite 621
   Memphis, TN 38104
   901-544-0115
   TTY: 901-544-0112

Miami District Office
   One Biscayne Tower
   2 South Biscayne Boulevard
   Suite 2700
   Miami, FL 33131
   305-536-4491
   TTY: 305-536-5721

Milwaukee District Office
   Reuss Federal Plaza
   310 West Wisconsin Avenue
   Suite 800
   Milwaukee, WI 53203-2292
   414-297-1111
   TTY: 414-297-1115

Minneapolis Area Office
   Towle Building
   330 South Second Avenue
   Suite 430
   Minneapolis, MN 55401-2224
   612-335-4040
   TTY: 612-335-4045

Nashville Area Office
   50 Vantage Way
   Suite 202
   Nashville, TN 37228-9940
   615-736-5820
   TTY: 615-736-5870

Newark Area Office
   One Newark Center
   Twenty-First Floor
   Newark, NJ 07102-5233
   973-645-6383
   TTY: 973-645-3004

New Orleans District Office
   701 Loyola Avenue
   Suite 600
   New Orleans, LA 70113-9936
   504-589-2329
   TTY: 504-589-2958

New York District Office
33 Whitehall Street
New York, NY 10004
212-336-3620
TTY: 212-336-3622

Norfolk Area Office
Federal Building
200 Granby Street
Suite 739
Norfolk, VA 23510
757-441-3470
TTY: 757-441-3578

Oakland Local Office
1301 Clay Street
Suite 1170-N
Oakland, CA 94612-5217
510-637-3230
TTY: 510-637-3234

Oklahoma Area Office
210 Park Avenue
Suite 1350
Oklahoma City, OK 73102
405-231-4911
TTY: 405-231-5745

Philadelphia District Office
The Bourse Building
21 South Fifth Street
Fourth Floor
Philadelphia, PA 19106
215-440-2600
TTY: 215-440-2610

Phoenix District Office
3300 North Central Avenue
Suite 690
Phoenix, AZ 85012-2504
602-640-5000
TTY: 602-640-5072

Pittsburgh Area Office
1001 Liberty Avenue
Suite 300
Pittsburgh, PA 15222-4187
412-644-3444
TTY: 412-644-2720

Raleigh Area Office
1309 Annapolis Drive
Raleigh, NC 27608-2129
919-856-4064
TTY: 919-856-4296

Richmond Area Office
  830 East Main Street
  Sixth Floor
  Richmond, VA 23219
  804-771-2200
  TTY: 804-771-2227

San Antonio District Office
  Mockingbird Plaza II
  5410 Fredericksburg Road
  Suite 200
  San Antonio, TX 78229
  210-281-7600
  TTY: 210-281-7610

San Diego Area Office
  Wells Fargo Bank Building
  401 B. Street
  Suite 510
  San Diego, CA 92101
  619-557-7235
  TTY: 619-557-5748

San Francisco District Office
  350 The Embarcadero
  Suite 500
  San Francisco, CA 94105-1260
  415-625-5600
  TTY: 415-625-5610

San Jose Local Office
    96 North Third Street
    Suite 200
    San Jose, CA 95112
    408-291-7352
    TTY: 408-291-7374

Savannah Local Office
    410 Mall Boulevard
    Suite G
    Savannah, GA 31406-4821
    912-652-4234
    TTY: 912-652-4439

Seattle District Office
    Federal Office Building
    909 First Avenue
    Suite 400
    Seattle, WA 98104-1061
    206-220-6883
    TTY: 206-220-6882

St. Louis District Office
    Robert A. Young Federal Building
    1222 Spruce Street
    Room 8.100
    St. Louis, MO 63103
    314-539-7800
    TTY: 314-539-7803

Tampa Area Office
501 East Polk Street
Suite 1000
Tampa, FL 33602
813-228-2310
TTY: 813-228-2003

Washington Field Office
1801 L Street, NW
Suite 100
Washington, DC 20507
202-419-0700
TTY: 202-419-0702

appendix b:
Title VII of the Civil Rights Act

Law: 42 U.S.C. Sec. 2000e.

Scope: Employers with at least fifteen employees who work at least twenty weeks a year, but excludes bona fide nonprofit, private membership clubs.

Covers: Among other things, Title VII prohibits employment discrimination based sex. It is an unlawful employment practice for an employer (1) to fail or refuse to hire or to discharge or otherwise to discriminate against any individual with respect to his compensation, terms, conditions, or privileges of employment, because of such individual's sex; or (2) to limit, segregate, or classify employees or applicants for employment that deprives them of employment opportunities, or otherwise adversely affects their status as employees, because of sex. It is also unlawful for an employment agency to fail or refuse to refer for employment, or otherwise to discriminate against, any individual because of sex or refer for employment any individual on the basis of his sex. Also prohibited is sex discrimination in apprenticeship or other training or retraining, including on-the-job training programs. However, there is an exception where sex is a bona fide occupational qualification that is reasonably necessary to the normal operation of the particular business.

Retaliation for filing a charge or cooperating in the investigation of a charge is also prohibited.

Remedies: Hiring, reinstatement, promotion, back pay, temporary restraining orders, attorneys fees, and other appropriate relief.

Agency: Equal Employment Opportunity Commission (EEOC)
1801 L. Street NW
Washington, DC 20507
800-669-4000
TTY: 800-669-6820

The EEOC enforces federal antidiscrimination laws. The EEOC's contact center has representatives in one hundred different languages.

appendix c:
State-by-State Fair Employment Practices Laws and Antidiscrimination Enforcement Agencies

This Appendix includes a state-by-state summary of the sexual harassment laws and agencies designed to enforce them. The summaries include the law citation, so you can read the actual law of your state using the legal research strategies of Chapter 12. The summaries also include the scope of each law and who is covered under the law provisions. If remedies are provided, those are listed as well. Finally, agency contact information is provided.

NOTE: *The sexual harassment laws do change. You should check with your state or federal agency to get the latest update on the law for your state as soon as practicable, so you will have time to decide on a plan of action.*

ALABAMA

NOTE: *Alabama does not have a specific statute on sexual harassment nor a state agency for filing claims. Except as below, claims should be filed with the EEOC.*

Law: Code of Alabama, Section 29-4-3.

Scope: Applies to employees of the Legislature.

Covers: In the selection of the employees of the Legislature, there shall be no discrimination on account of sex. (Sec. 29-4-3.)

Remedies: None listed.

Agency: Alabama Department of Human Resources (for covered workers only)

Office of Equal Employment and Civil Rights
50 North Ripley Street
Montgomery, AL 36130
334-242-1310

All others: Contact EEOC (see Appendix A)

ALASKA

Law: Alaska Statutes, Sections 18.80.010 to 18.80.300.

Scope: Public and private employers, employment agencies, labor organizations, communications media, but not domestic workers, social clubs, or not-for-profits. (Secs. 18.80.220 and 18.80.300.)

Covers: It is unlawful for an employer to refuse to hire or discriminate in compensation, term, condition, or privilege of employment because of a person's sex. (Sec. 18.80.220.)

Remedies: Hiring, reinstatement, promotion, back pay, temporary restraining orders, attorney's fees, other appropriate relief.

Agency: Human Rights Commission
800 A Street
Suite 204
Anchorage, AK 99501
800-478-3177
www.gov.state.ak.us/aschr

ARIZONA

Law: Arizona Revised Statutes Annotated, Sections 41-1461 to 1466, 41-1481 to 1485.

Scope: State and private employers, employment agencies, labor organizations, certain staff of elected officials, or private nonprofit membership clubs. (Sec. 41-1461.)

Covers: It is unlawful for an employer to fail or refuse to hire or to discharge or otherwise discriminate against any individual regarding compensation, terms, conditions, or privileges of employment on the basis of sex. (Sec. 41-1463.)

Remedies: Hiring, reinstatement, promotion, back pay, temporary restraining orders, attorney's fees to prevailing party, other appropriate relief.

Agency: Office of Equal Opportunity
State Capitol Building
1700 West Washington
Suite 156
Phoenix, AZ 85007
602-364-4386
www.azgovernor.go/eop

ARKANSAS

Law: Arkansas Code Annotated.

Scope: Applies to state employees. (Sec. 21-12-103.)

Covers: Every state agency shall include in its personnel manual a statement that discrimination by any officer or employee based upon sex shall constitute grounds for dismissal. When it is determined by any court of law that any employee of this state is guilty of discrimination based upon sex, it is grounds for dismissal from employment. (Sec. 1-12-103 (a),(b).)

Remedies: None listed.

Agency: Contact EEOC (see Appendix A)

CALIFORNIA

Law: West's Annotated California codes, Government Code. Fair Employment Practices and Housing Act, Sections 12900 to 12996.

Scope: Public and private employers, employment agencies, labor organizations employing five or more employees, but not certain family members or non-profit religious organizations. (Secs. 12926 and 12940.)

Covers: The opportunity to seek and obtain and hold employment without discrimination because of sex is a civil right. (Sec. 12921.) It is an unlawful employment practice, unless based on a bona fide occupational qualification or applicable security regulations, for an employer, because of sex, to refuse to hire or employ the person or to refuse to select the person for a training program leading to employment or to bar or discharge any the person from employment or from a training program leading to employment or to discriminate against the person in compensation or in terms, conditions, or privileges of employment. (Sec. 12940.) Requires the employer to ensure a workplace free of sexual harassment by posting information on the illegality of sexual harassment and retaliation and providing information individually to employees listing descriptions of sexually harassing conduct and the employer's internal complaint process as well as methods for filing a complaint with the state's fair employment practice agency. (Sec. 12950.)

Remedies: Hiring, reinstatement, promotion, back pay, temporary restraining orders, cease and desist orders, attorney's fees, other appropriate relief such as monetary damages.

Agency: Department of Fair Employment and Housing
2000 O Street
Suite 120
Sacramento, CA 95814
800-884-1684
TTY: 800-700-2320
www.dfeh.ca.gov

COLORADO

Law: West's Colorado Revised Statutes Annotated, Sections
            24-34-301 to -406.

Scope: Public and private employers, employment agencies,
            labor organizations, but not domestic workers or tax
            exempt religious organizations. (Sec. 4-34-401.)

Covers: It is a discriminatory employment practice for an
            employer to refuse to hire, discharge, promote or
            demote, to harass or to discriminate in compensation
            against any qualified person on the basis of sex. To
            harass includes to create a hostile work environment
            based on a person's sex. (Sec. 24-34-402.)

Remedies: Hiring, reinstatement, promotion, back pay, cease
            and desist order.

Agency: Colorado Civil Rights Division Central Office
            1560 Broadway
            Suite 1050
            Denver, CO 80202
            800-262-4845
            www.dora.state.co.us/civil-rights

CONNECTICUT

Law: Connecticut General Statutes Annotated, Sections 46a-51 to -99. Fair Employment Practices Act.

Scope: Public and private employers, employment agencies, labor organizations, but not employers of less than three workers, domestic or family workers. (Sec. 46a-51.)

Covers: It is a discriminatory practice for an employer or its agent to refuse to hire or to bar or fire any person or to discriminate in compensation, terms, conditions, or privileges of employment because of sex or to sexually harass an applicant or an employee. (Sec. 46a-60.)

Remedies: Hiring, reinstatement, promotion, back pay (less interim earnings), temporary restraining orders (applies to employers of fifty or more), cease and desist orders and other appropriate relief.

Agency: Connecticut Commission on Human Rights and Opportunities
21 Grand Street
Hartford, CT 06106
860-541-3400
TDD: 860-541-3459
www.state.ct.us/chro

DELAWARE

Law: Delaware Code Annotated, Title 19, Sections 710-
718.

Scope: Public and private employers, employment agencies, labor organizations, but not employers of less
than four workers; domestic, agricultural, or family
workers; or, private charitable organizations. (Secs.
710 and 711.)

Covers: It shall be an unlawful employment practice for an
employer to fail or refuse to hire or to discharge any
person or otherwise discriminate on the basis of
compensation, terms, conditions, or privileges of
employment because of sex. (Sec. 711.)

Remedies: Hiring, reinstatement, promotion, back pay (less
interim earnings), cease and desist order, attorney's
fees to prevailing party and other appropriate relief.

Agency: Delaware Department of Labor
Office of Labor Law Enforcement
4425 North Market Street
P.O. Box 9954
Wilmington, DE 19802
302-761-8200
www.delaware.gov

DISTRICT OF COLUMBIA

Law: District of Columbia Code Ann. Sections 2-1401.01 to
2-1403.17.

Scope: Government and private employers, employment
agencies, labor organizations, but not domestic or
family workers. (Sec. 2-1401.02.)

Covers: It is an unlawful discriminatory practice to fail or
refuse to hire, or to discharge any individual or to
otherwise discriminate against any person because
of compensation, terms, conditions, or privileges of
employment including promotion, deprivation of
employment opportunities, or adverse affect on an
individual's employment status on the basis of sex.
(Sec. 2-1402.11.)

Remedies: Hiring, reinstatement, promotion, back pay, temporary restraining orders, cease and desist order,
money damages, attorney's fees, other appropriate
relief.

Agency: District of Columbia Office of Human Rights
441 4th Street, NW
Suite 570 North
Washington, DC 20001
202-727-4559
www.ohr.dc.gov

FLORIDA

Law: Florida Statutes Annotated, Sections 760.01 to 760.11.

Scope: Public and private employers, employment agencies, labor organizations, employers with less than fifteen workers. (Secs. 60.02 and 760.10.)

Covers: It is an unlawful employment practice for an employer to discharge, or fail or refuse to hire any person or otherwise discriminate against any individual with respect to compensation, terms, conditions, or privileges of employment because of sex. It is also unlawful to deprive applicants or employees of employment opportunities or to adversely affect employee status. (Sec. 760.10.)

Remedies: Appropriate affirmative action, back pay, cease and desist orders, attorney's fees.

Agency: Florida Commission on Human Relations
2009 Apalachee Parkway
Suite 100
Tallahassee, FL 32301
800-342-8170
TDD ASCII: 800-955-1339
TDD Baudot: 800-955-8771
http://fchr.state.fl.us

GEORGIA

NOTE: *Georgia does not have a specific statute on sexual harassment nor a state agency for filing claims. Except as below, claims should be filed with the EEOC.*

Law: Official Code of Georgia Annotated, Sections 45-19-20 to 45-19-45.

Scope: Public employers which employ at least fifteen workers or staff of public officials. (Sec. 45-19-22.)

Covers: It is an unlawful employment practice for an employer to fail or refuse to hire, to discharge, or otherwise to discriminate against any person regarding compensation, term, conditions, privileges of employment because of sex. It is also unlawful to segregate or classify employees to deprive employment opportunities or otherwise adversely affect employment status. (Sec. 45-19-29.)

Remedies: Hiring, reinstatement, promotion, back pay (less interim earnings), cease and desist orders, actual money damages, attorney's fees to prevailing party if case goes to court, other appropriate relief.

Agency: Georgia Commission on Equal Opportunity
2 Martin Luther King, Jr. Drive
Suite 1002
West Tower
229 Peachtree Street, SE
Atlanta, GA 30334
800-473-OPEN
www.gceo.state.ga.us

All others: Contact EEOC (see Appendix A)

HAWAII

Law: Hawaii Revised Statutes, Sections 378-1 to -38. Hawaii Fair Employment Practices Act.

Scope: Public and private employers, employment agencies, labor organizations, but not domestic workers. (Sec. 378-1.)

Covers: It is an unlawful discriminatory practice where because of sex an employer refuses to hire, employ or bars or discharges an employee or otherwise discriminates in compensation, terms, conditions, or privileges of employment. It is also unlawful for any person to aid, abet, incite, compel or coerce the doing of any discriminatory practice. (Sec. 378-1.)

Remedies: Hiring, reinstatement, back pay, injunctions, cease and desist orders, attorney's fees to prevailing plaintiffs, other appropriate relief.

NOTE: *Where judgment is not paid within thirty days, court can order a respondent to close business until judgment is paid.*

Agency: Hawaii Civil Rights Commission
830 Punchbowl Street
Room 411
Honolulu, HI 96813
808-586-8636
TDD: 808-586-8692
http://hawaii.gov/labor/hcrc

IDAHO

Law: Idaho Code Ann. Sections 67-5901 to 67-5911.

Scope: Public and private employers, employment agencies, labor organizations, but not employers with less than five workers. (Secs. 67-5902 and 67-5908.)

Covers: It is prohibited to discriminate against a person because of sex. It is prohibited for an employer to fire or refuse to hire, to discharge, or to otherwise discriminate against a person with respect to compensation, terms, conditions, privileges of employment or to reduce the wage or an employee to comply with the law. It is also prohibited to classify or segregate so as to limit employment opportunities or to adversely affect status of an employee or to cause or attempt to cause an employer to violate the antidiscrimination law. (Sec. 67-5909.)

Remedies: Hiring, reinstatement, promotion, back pay, cease and desist orders, actual damages, other appropriate relief.

Agency: Idaho Commission on Human Rights
1109 Main Street
Suite 400
P.O. Box 83720
Boise, ID 83720-0040
888-249-7025
TDD: 208-334-4751
www.state.id.us/ihrc

ILLINOIS

Law: West's Illinois Compiled Statutes Annotated. 775 ILCS 5/1-101 to 5/10-102 Illinois Human Rights Act; also ILCS Const. Art. I, Section 18.

Scope: Public and private employers, employment agencies, labor organizations, but not domestic or certain vocational workers, religious organizations, public officials and staffs. (Sec. 5/2-101.)

Covers: It is a civil rights violation for any employer to refuse to hire, to segregate, or to act with respect to recruitment, hiring, promotion, renewal of employment, selection for training or apprenticeship, discharge, discipline, tenure or terms, privileges, or conditions of employment on the basis of sex. Sexual harassment means any unwelcome sexual advances or requests for sexual favors or any conduct of a sexual nature when (1) submission to such conduct is made either explicitly or implicitly a term or condition of an individual's employment; (2) submission to or rejection of such conduct by an individual is used as the basis for employment decisions affecting such individual; or, (3) such conduct has the purpose or effect of substantially interfering with an individual's work performance or creating an intimidating, hostile or offensive working environment. (Secs. 5/2-101 and 5/2-102.)

Remedies: Hiring, reinstatement, promotion, back pay, temporary restraining and cease and desist orders, actual
damages, attorney's fees, other appropriate relief.

Agency: Illinois Department of Human Rights
James R. Thompson Center
100 West Randolph
Suite 10-100
Chicago, IL 60601
312-814-6200
TDD: 312-263-1579
www.state.il.us/dhr

INDIANA

Law: Burns Ind. Code Annotated, Sections 22-9-1-2 to 22-9-1-13.

Scope: Public and private employers, employment agencies, labor organizations, but not employers with less than six workers, domestic or certain family workers, social, nonprofit, or religious organizations. (Sec. 22-9-1-3.)

Covers: It is the policy of this state to provide all citizens with equal opportunities for employment. (Sec. 22-9-1-2.) The exclusion of a person from equal opportunities because of sex is an unlawful discriminatory practice unless based on a bona fide occupational qualification which is reasonably necessary to the normal operation of the business. (Sec. 22-9-1-3.)

Remedies: Affirmative action, including back pay, cease and desist orders, other appropriate relief.

Agency: The Indiana Civil Rights Commission
            Indiana Government Center North
            100 North Senate Avenue
            Room N103
            Indianapolis, IN 46204
            800-628-2909
            TDD: 800-743-3333
            www.state.in.us/icrc

IOWA

Law: Iowa Code Annotated, Section 216. Iowa Civil Rights
Act.

Scope: Public and private employers, employment agencies,
labor organizations, but not employers with less than
four workers, domestic or certain family workers.
(Secs. 216.2 and 216.6.)

Covers: It is an unfair or discriminatory practice for any person to refuse to hire, accept, register, classify or refer
for employment, to discharge any employee, or to
otherwise discriminate in employment against any
applicant because of sex, unless based on the nature
of the occupation.

Remedies: Hiring, reinstatement, promotion, back pay (less
interim earnings), actual damages, attorney's fees,
other appropriate relief.

Agency: Iowa Civil Rights Commission
Grimes State Office Building
400 East 14th Street
Des Moines, IA 50319-1004
800-457-4416
www.state.ia.us/government/crc

KANSAS

Law: Kansas Statutes Annotated, Sections 44-1001 to -1311. Kansas Act Against Discrimination.

Scope: Public and private employers, employment agencies, labor and social service organizations, but not employers with less than four workers, domestic or certain family workers, or social or nonprofit organizations. (Sec. 44-1002.)

Covers: It is an unlawful employment practice for an employer, because of sex, to refuse to hire or employ such person to bar or discharge such person from employment or to otherwise discriminate against such person in compensation, terms, conditions, or privileges of employment; to limit segregate, separate, classify or make any distinction in regards to employees; or, to follow any employment procedure or practice which results in discrimination without a valid business necessity. (Sec. 44-1009.)

Remedies: Hiring, reinstatement, promotion, back pay, cease and desist orders, certain pain and suffering damages and actual damages, other appropriate relief.

Agency: Kansas Human Rights Commission
900 SW Jackson
Suite 568-5
Topeka, KS 66612-1258
785-296-3206
TTY: 785-296-0245
www.khrc.net

KENTUCKY

Law: Kentucky Revised Statutes Annotated, Sections 344.010-500, 344.207.170. Chapter 344. Civil Rights.

Scope: Employers, employment agencies, labor organizations, but not employers with less than eight workers, domestic or certain family workers. (Secs. 344.020 and 344.010-.070.)

Covers: It is an unlawful practice for an employer to fail or refuse to hire, or to discharge any individual, or otherwise to discriminate against an individual with respect to compensation, terms, conditions, or privileges of employment because of the individual's sex. (Sec. 344.040.)

Remedies: Hiring, reinstatement, promotion, back pay (less interim earnings), temporary restraining and cease and desist orders, damages, attorney's fees, other appropriate relief.

Agency: Kentucky Commission on Human Rights
332 West Broadway
Suite 700
Louisville, KY 40202
800-292-5566
TDD: 502-595-4084
www.state.ky.us/agencies2/kchr

LOUISIANA

Law: West's Louisiana Statutes Annotated, Section 23-301-340. Louisiana Employment Discrimination Law.

Scope: Public and private employers, employment agencies, labor organizations, but not employers with less than twenty workers, religious, or nonprofit organizations. (Sec. 23-302.)

Covers: It is unlawful for an employer to intentionally fail or refuse to hire, or to discharge any individual, or otherwise intentionally discriminate against an individual with respect to his or her compensation or his or her terms, conditions, or privileges of employment because of the individual's sex unless as a result of a bona fide occupational qualification reasonably necessary for the normal operation of business. (Sec. 23-332.)

Remedies: Hiring, reinstatement, promotion, back pay, damages, attorney's fees, other appropriate relief.

Agency: Louisiana Commission on Human Rights
1001 North 23rd Street
Suite 262
P.O. Box 94094
Baton Rouge, LA 70802
225-342-6969
TDD: 888-248-0859
www.gov.state.la.us/depts/lchr.htm

MAINE

Law: Maine Revised Statutes Annotated, title V, Sections 4551 to 4632. Maine Human Rights Act.

Scope: Public and private employers and their agents, employment agencies, labor organizations, but not certain family workers. (Secs. 4553 and 4572.)

Covers: It is unlawful employment discrimination for any employer to fail or refuse to hire or otherwise discriminate against any applicant for employment or to discharge an employee or discriminate with respect to hire, tenure, promotion, transfer, compensation, terms, conditions, or privileges of employment or any other matter directly or indirectly related to employment because of sex, unless based on a bona fide occupational qualification. (Sec. 4572.)

Remedies: Reinstatement, back pay, temporary restraining, and cease and desist orders, attorney's fees, other appropriate relief.

Agency: Maine Human Rights Commission
51 State House Station
Augusta, ME 04333-0051
207-624-6050
TTY/TTD: 888-577-6690
www.state.me.us/mhrc

MARYLAND

Law: Annotated Code of Maryland, art. 49b, Sections 14–18. Fair Employment Practices Act.

Scope: Public and private employers, employment agencies, labor organizations, but not employers with less than fifteen workers, staffs of public officials and membership clubs. (Secs. 15 and 16.)

Covers: It is an unlawful employment practice for an employer to fail or refuse to hire or to discharge an individual or otherwise to discriminate against any individual with respect to the individual's compensation, terms, conditions, or privileges of employment because of such individual's sex, unless based on a bona fide occupational qualification. (Sec. 16.)

Remedies: Hiring, reinstatement, promotion, back pay, cease and desist orders, other appropriate relief.

Agency: Maryland Commission on Human Relations
William Donald Shaefer Towers
6 Saint Paul Street
Suite 900
Baltimore, MD 21202
800-637-6247
TTY: 410-333-1737
www.mchr.state.md.us

MASSACHUSETTS

Law: Annotated Laws of Massachusetts, Chapter 151B.,
             Sections 1–10. Massachusetts Fair Employment
             Practices Law.

Scope: Public and private employers and agents, employ-
             ment agencies, labor organizations, but not employ-
             ers with less than six workers, nonprofit
             organizations. (Secs. 1 and 4.)

Covers: It is an unlawful employment practice for an
             employer or an agent of the employer to refuse to
             hire or employ or to bar or to discharge from
             employment an individual or to discriminate
             against an individual in compensation, terms, con-
             ditions, or privileges of employment because of the
             individual's sex, unless based on a bona fide occu-
             pational qualification. It is also an unlawful
             employment practice for an employer, personally
             or through its agents, to sexually harass any
             employee. (Sec. 4.)

             NOTE: *Massachusetts has a specific statutory require-
             ment for employers to adopt a sexual harassment pol-
             icy and to provide the policy to employees. The policy
             must include descriptions and examples of what con-
             stitutes sexual harassment along with the process for
             filing internal complaints. (Sec. 3A.)*

Remedies: Hiring, reinstatement, promotion, back pay, cease
             and desist and temporary restraining orders, attor-
             ney's fees to prevailing party, other appropriate
             relief.

continued

Agency: Massachusetts Commission Against Discrimination
One Ashburton Place
Room 601
Boston, MA 02108
671-994-6000
www.mass.gov/mcad

MICHIGAN

Law: Michigan Compiled Laws Annotated, Sections 37.2101, 37.202. Elliott-Larsen Civil Rights Act.

Scope: Public and private employers, employment agencies, labor organizations, but not certain family workers. (Sec. 37.2202.)

Covers: An employer shall not fail or refuse to hire or recruit, discharge or otherwise discriminate against an individual with respect to employment, compensation, or a term, condition or privilege of employment because of sex. (Sec. 37.202.)

Remedies: Hiring, reinstatement, promotion, back pay, cease and desist orders, damages, attorney's fees, other appropriate relief.

Agency: Michigan Department of Civil Rights
Cadillac Place
3054 West Grand Boulevard
Suite 3-600
Detroit, MI 48202
313-456-3700
WATS: 800-482-3604
TTY: 877-878-8464
www.michigan.gov/mdcr

MINNESOTA

Law: Minnesota Statutes Annotated, Section 363.01–363.20. Human Rights.

Scope: Public and private employers, employment agencies, labor organizations, but not domestic and certain family workers. (Secs. 363.01 and 363.02.)

Covers: It is an unfair employment practice for an employer to refuse to hire or to maintain a system of employment which unreasonably excludes a person seeking employment or to discharge an employee or to discriminate against a person with respect to hiring, tenure, compensation, terms, upgrading, conditions facilities or privileges of employment because of such individual's sex, unless based on a bona fide occupational qualification. (Sec. 363.03.) Sexual harassment includes unwanted sexual advances, requests for sexual favors, sexually motivated physical contact or other verbal or physical conduct or communication of a sexual nature when submission to that conduct is made a factor in decision making concerning that individual's employment or substantially interferes with an individual's employment. (Sec. 363.01.subd.41.)

Remedies: Hiring, reinstatement, promotion, back pay, cease and desist orders, damages, attorney's fees to prevailing party, other appropriate relief.

Agency: Department of Human Rights
190 East 5th Street
Suite 700
St. Paul, MN 55101
800-657-3704
TTY: 651-296-1283
www.humanrights.state.mn.us

MISSISSIPPI

NOTE: *Mississippi does not have a specific statute on sexual harassment nor a state agency for filing claims. Except as below, claims should be filed with the EEOC.*

Law: Mississippi Code Annotated, Section 25-9-149.

Scope: Applies to employees in state government.

Covers: No person seeking employment in state service or employed in state service shall be discriminated against on the basis of sex. (Sec. 25-9-149.)

Remedies: None stated.

Agency: Contact EEOC (see Appendix A)

MISSOURI

Law: Vernon's Annotated Missouri Statutes Sections 213.010–.130. Missouri Fair Employment Practices Act and Missouri Code of Regulations Section 60-3.040(17).

Scope: Public and private employers, employment agencies, labor organizations, but not employers with less than six workers or religious organizations. (Secs. 213.055 and 213.010.)

Covers: It is an unlawful employment practice for an employer to fail or refuse to hire or to discharge an individual or otherwise to discriminate against any individual with respect to the individual's compensation, terms, conditions, or privileges of employment because of such individual's sex, or to limit or classify employees or applicants to deprive or tend to deprive them of employment opportunities on the basis of sex. Certain exceptions apply based on a bona fide occupational qualification. (Sec. 213.055.)

Remedies: Hiring, reinstatement, promotion, back pay, cease and desist and temporary restraining orders, money damages, attorney's fees for prevailing parties, other appropriate relief.

Agency: Missouri Commission on Human Rights
P.O. Box 1129
3315 West Truman Boulevard
Jefferson City, MO 65102-1129
573-751-3325
www.dolir.state.mo.us/hr

MONTANA

Law: Montana Code Annotated, Sections 49-1-101 to 49-2-601. Montana Human Rights Act.

Scope: Public and private employers, employment agencies, labor organizations, but not certain not-for-profit agencies. (Secs. 49-2-303 and 308, 49-2-101.)

Covers: It is an unlawful discriminatory practice for an employer to refuse employment to a person, to bar a person from employment, or to discriminate against a person in compensation, or in a term, condition, or privilege of employment because of sex, when the reasonable demands of the position do not require a sex distinction. (Sec. 49-2-303.)

Remedies: Reasonable measures to correct the discrimination and harm caused, cease and desist orders, temporary orders, attorney's fees to prevailing parties under certain circumstances. Does not allow punitive damages.

Agency: Montana Human Rights Bureau
            1625 11ᵗʰ Avenue
            P.O. Box 1728
            Helena, MT 59624-1728
            800-542-0807
            http://erd.dli.state.mt.us/HumanRight/HRhome.htm

NEBRASKA

Law: Revised Statutes of Nebraska, Sections 48-1101 to
              -1126. Nebraska Fair Employment Act.

Scope: Public and private employers, employment agencies,
              labor organizations, but not employers with less than
              fifteen workers, domestic and certain family workers,
              and tax-exempt private membership clubs. (Secs. 48-
              1102, 48-1104, and 48-1106.)

Covers: It is an unlawful employment practice for an
              employer to refuse employment, to fail or refuse to
              hire, to discharge or to harass any individual, or oth-
              erwise to discriminate against any individual with
              respect to compensation, terms, conditions, or privi-
              leges of employment because of sex, or to limit,
              solicit or advertise, or classify employees on the
              basis of sex when to do so would limit or deprive
              any individual of employment opportunities or status
              as an employee. (Sec. 48-1104.)

Remedies: Hiring, reinstatement, promotion, back pay (from
              which interim earnings are deducted), cease and
              desist orders, attorney's fees if case goes to court,
              other appropriate relief.

Agency: Nebraska Equal Opportunity Commission
              Nebraska State Office Building
              301 Centennial Mall South
              Fifth Floor
              P.O. Box 94934
              Lincoln, NE 68509-4934
              800-642-6112
              www.nol.org/home/NEOC

NEVADA

Law: Nevada Revised Statutes Annotated. (Sections 613.310
             to 613.430.) Nevada Fair Employment Practices Act.

Scope: Public and private employers, employment agencies,
             labor organizations, but not employers with less than
             fifteen workers, tax-exempt, private membership
             clubs. (Secs. 13.330 and 613.310.)

Covers: It is an unlawful employment practice for an
             employer to fail or refuse to hire, or to discharge any
             person, or otherwise to discriminate against any per-
             son with respect to his compensation, terms, condi-
             tions, or privileges of employment because of sex
             unless on the basis of a bona fide occupational qual-
             ification reasonably necessary to the normal opera-
             tion of that particular business. (Sec. 613.350.)

Remedies: Hiring, reinstatement, back pay, and other appropri-
             ate remedies, including interest on lost wages, cease
             and desist orders, temporary relief orders.

Agency: Nevada Equal Rights Commission
             Las Vegas Office:
             1515 East Tropicana Avenue
             Suite 590
             Las Vegas, NV 89119-6522
             702-486-7161
             TDD: 702-486-7164
             http://detr.state.nv.us/nerc/NERC_index.htm

             Reno Office:
             1325 Corporate Boulevard
             Reno, NV 89502
             775-688-1288

NEW HAMPSHIRE

Law: New Hampshire Statutes Annotated Sections 354-A:1
to A:25. New Hampshire Law Against Discrimination.

Scope: Public and private employers, employment agencies,
labor organizations, but not employers with less than
six workers, domestic and certain family workers,
social clubs, or nonprofit. (Secs. 354-A:7 and 354-A:2.)

Covers: It is an unlawful discriminatory practice for an
employer because of sex to refuse to hire, employ or
to bar or to discharge from employment, or to discriminate against an individual in compensation, or
in terms, conditions, or privileges of employment
because of sex, unless the bona fide demands of the
position require a sex distinction. (Sec. 354-A:7(I).)
Sexual harassment constitutes sex discrimination.
Unwelcome sexual advances, requests for sexual
favors, and other verbal, non-verbal or physical conduct of a sexual nature constitutes sexual harassment
when: (a) submission to such conduct is made either
explicitly or implicitly a term or condition of an individual's employment; (b) submission to or rejection
of such conduct by an individual is used as the basis
for employment decisions affecting such individual;
or, (c) such conduct has the purpose or effect of
unreasonably interfering with an individual's work
performance or creating an intimidating, hostile, or
offensive working environment. (Sec. 354-A:7(V).)

continued

Remedies: Hiring, reinstatement, promotion, back pay (from which interim earnings are deducted), cease and desist orders, compensatory damages, attorney's fees, other appropriate relief.

Agency: New Hampshire Commission for Human Rights
2 Chenell Drive
Concord, NH 03301-8501
603-271-2767
www.state.nh.us/hrc

NEW JERSEY

Law: New Jersey Statutes Annotated Sections 10:5-1 to 10:5-42. New Jersey Law Against Discrimination.

Scope: Public and private employers, employment agencies, labor organizations, but not domestic workers. (Secs. 10:5-5 and 10:5-12.)

Covers: It is an unlawful employment practice for an employer, because of sex, to refuse to hire or employ or to bar or to discharge an individual from employment, or to discriminate against an individual in compensation, or in terms, conditions, or privileges of employment because of sex, when the reasonable demands of the position do not require a sex distinction. (Sec. 10:5-12(a).)

Remedies: Hiring, reinstatement, promotion, cease and desist orders, attorney's fees to prevailing parties (to defendant only if case is brought in bad faith), other appropriate relief.

Agency: New Jersey Division on Civil Rights
140 East Front Street
P.O. Box 090
Trenton, NJ 08625-0090
609-292-4605
www.state.nj.us/lps/dcr

NEW MEXICO

Law: New Mexico Statutes Annotated, Sections 28-1-1 to 28-1-14. New Mexico Human Rights Act.

Scope: Public and private employers, employment agencies, labor organizations, but not employers with less than four workers. (Secs. 28-1-2 and 28-1-7.)

Covers: It is an unlawful discriminatory practice for an employer to refuse to hire, to discharge, to promote or demote or to discriminate in matters of compensation, terms, conditions, or privileges of employment because of sex, unless statutorily prohibited or the reasonable demands of the position require a sex distinction. (Sec. 28-1-7(a).)

Remedies: Any necessary affirmative action (such as hiring, reinstatement, promotion, back pay, actual damages), cease and desist and other injunctive orders, attorney's fees, other appropriate relief.

Agency: New Mexico Human Rights Division
             1596 Pacheco Street
             Santa Fe, NM 87505
             800-566-9471
             www.dol.state.nm.us/dol_hrd.html

NEW YORK

Law: McKinney's Consolidated Laws of New York
            Annotated, Executive Law, (Secs. 290–301.) New
            York Human Rights Law.

Scope: Employers, licensing agencies, employment agen-
            cies, labor organizations, but not employers with less
            than four workers, domestic or certain family workers.
            (Secs. 292 and 296.)

Covers: It is an unlawful discriminatory practice for an
            employer, because of sex, to refuse to hire or employ
            or to bar or discharge a person from employment, or
            to discriminate against an individual in compensation,
            or in terms, conditions, or privileges of employment
            when the reasonable demands of the position do not
            require a sex distinction. (Sec. 296(1).)

Remedies: Hiring, reinstatement, promotion, back pay, cease
            and desist orders, temporary relief, compensatory
            damages, other appropriate relief.

Agency: Office of Sexual Harassment
            Division of Human Rights
            One Fordham Plaza
            Bronx, NY 10458
            718-741-8400
            www.dhr.state.ny.us

NORTH CAROLINA

Law: North Carolina General Statutes, Sections 143-422.1 to 422.3. North Carolina Equal Employment Practices Act.

Scope: Employers, but not employers with less than fifteen workers. (Sec. 143-422.2.)

Covers: The public policy of North Carolina is that persons have a right to seek employment without discrimination on the basis of sex. (Sec. 143.422.2.) Discrimination on the basis of sex and sexual harassment are against the public policy of North Carolina.

Remedies: Appropriate affirmative relief.

Agency: EEOC (see Appendix A)
              www.oah.state.nc.us/civil

NORTH DAKOTA

Law: North Dakota Century Code Annotated Sections 14-
02.4-01   to   14-02.4-21.   North   Dakota   Fair
Employment Practices Act.

Scope: Employers, employment agencies, labor organizations, but not employers with employees for less
than one-quarter of a year, domestic and certain family workers and political staff. (Secs. 14-02.4-03, 14-
02.4-02, and 14-02.4-10.)

Covers: It is a discriminatory practice for an employer to fail
or refuse to hire a person or to discharge an
employee or to accord adverse or unequal treatment
to a person or employee with respect to application,
hiring, training, apprenticeship, tenure, promotion,
upgrading, compensation, layoff, or a term, privilege, or condition of employment because of sex,
unless due to a bona fide occupational qualification
reasonably necessary to the normal operation of that
particular business. (Secs. 14-02.4-03 and 14-02.4-08.)
Specifically makes sexual harassment a form of sex
discrimination. Defines sexual harassment as: unwelcome sexual advances, requests for sexual favors,
sexually motivated physical conduct or other verbal
or physical conduct or communication of a sexual
nature when: (a) submission to that conduct is made
a term or condition, either explicitly or implicitly, of
obtaining employment; (b) submission to or rejection of that conduct or communication by an individual is used as a factor in decisions affecting that

continued

individual's employment; or, (c) that conduct or communication has the purpose or effect of substantially interfering with an individual's employment. (Sec. 14-02.4-02.(5).)

Remedies: Back pay (from which interim earnings are deducted), temporary relief orders, attorney's fees (prevailing party), other appropriate relief.

Agency: Division of Human Rights
600 East Boulevard Avenue
Department 406
Bismark, ND 58505-0340
800-582-8032
www.state.nd.us/labor/services/human-rights

OHIO

Law: Page's Ohio Revised Code Annotated, Sections
4112.01–.99. Ohio Fair Employment Practices Law.

Scope: Public and private employers, employment agencies,
labor organizations, but not employers with less than
four workers, domestic workers. (Secs. 4112.01 and
4112.02.)

Covers: It is an unlawful discriminatory practice for an
employer, because of sex, to discharge without
cause, to refuse to hire or otherwise to discriminate
against that person with respect to hire, tenure,
terms, conditions, or privileges of employment or in
any matter directly or indirectly related to employment unless based on a bona fide occupational qualification. (Sec. 4112.02(A),(E).)

Remedies: Hiring, reinstatement, promotion, back pay (from
which interim earnings may be deducted), cease and
desist orders, other appropriate relief.

Agency: Ohio Civil Rights Commission
Columbus Central Office
1111 East Broad Street
Suite 301
Columbus, OH 43205-1379
614-466-5928
TTY 614-753-2391
http://crc.ohio.gov

OKLAHOMA

Law: Oklahoma Statutes Annotated, Title 25, Section 1101-1802. Oklahoma Civil Rights Act.

Scope: Public and private employers, employment agencies, labor organizations, but not employers with less than fifteen workers, domestic and certain family workers, nonprofit membership clubs. (Secs. 1301 and 1302.)

Covers: It is an unlawful discriminatory practice for an employer to refuse to hire to discharge or otherwise to discriminate against an individual with respect to compensation, or the terms, conditions, privileges, or responsibilities of employment because of sex, unless related to a bona fide occupational qualification which is reasonably necessary to the normal operations of the employer's business. (Sec. 1302(A)(1).)

Remedies: Hiring, reinstatement, promotion, back pay (from which interim earnings are deducted), cease and desist orders, attorney's fees under certain circumstances, other appropriate relief.

Agency: Oklahoma Human Rights Commission
Jim Thorpe Building
2101 North Lincoln Boulevard
Room 480
Oklahoma City, OK 73105-4904
405-521-2360
TDD 405-522-3635
www.hrc.state.ok.us

OREGON

Law: Oregon Revised Statutes Annotated, Section 659.010
to 659.990. Oregon Fair Employment Practices Act.

Scope: Public and private employers, employment agencies,
labor organizations, but not domestic or certain family workers. (Secs. 659.010 and 659.030.)

Covers: It is an unlawful employment practice for an
employer, because of sex, to refuse to hire or
employ or to bar or discharge from employment
such individual unless related to a bona fide occupational qualification which is reasonably necessary
to the normal operations of the employer's business.
(Sec. 659.030(1)(a).)

Remedies: Hiring, reinstatement, promotion, back pay, cease
and desist orders, temporary relief orders, attorney's
fees to prevailing party, other appropriate relief.

Agency: Oregon Civil Rights Division
Bureau of Labor and Industries
800 NE Oregon Street
Suite 1045
Portland, OR 97232
971-673-0761
www.boli.state.or.us/civil

PENNSYLVANIA

Law: Purdon's Pennsylvania Consolidated Statutes Annotated, Title 43, Sections 951–955.

Scope: Public and private employers, employment agencies, labor organizations, but not employers with less than four workers, domestic or certain family workers, religious organizations, or agricultural workers. (Secs. 954 and 955.)

Covers: It is an unlawful discriminatory practice, unless based upon a bona fide occupational qualification, for an employer, because of sex, to refuse to hire or employ or to bar or to discharge from employment or otherwise to discriminate against such individual with respect to compensation, hire, tenure, terms, conditions, privileges of employment if that person is able and competent to perform the services required. (Sec. 955(a).) There are specific guidelines on sexual harassment which define how the human rights commission defines and investigates sexual harassment cases. (Human Relations Commission Guidelines on Sexual Harassment, 11 Pa. Bull. No.5 (Jan. 31, 1981).)

Remedies: Hiring, reinstatement, promotion, back pay, cease and desist orders, attorney's fees to prevailing party if case goes to court, other appropriate relief.

Agency: Pennsylvania Human Relations Commission
301 Chestnut Street
Suite 300
Harrisburg, PA 17101
717-787-4410
TTY: 717-787-4087
www.phrc.state.pa.us

RHODE ISLAND

Law: General laws of Rhode Island, Sections 28-5-1 to 28-5-39.

Scope: Public and private employers, employment agencies, labor organizations, but not employers with less than four workers, domestic and certain family workers. (Secs. 28-5-6 and 28-5-7.)

Covers: It is an unlawful employment practice for an employer to refuse to hire any applicant because of sex or to discharge or discriminate against an employee with respect to hire, tenure, compensation, terms, conditions, or privileges of employment, or any other matter directly or indirectly related to employment. (Sec. 28-5-7(1)(i).)

Remedies: Hiring, reinstatement, promotion, back pay (including all raises and benefits to which the employee would have been entitled), cease and desist orders, temporary restraining orders, money damages, attorney's fees to prevailing plaintiffs, other appropriate relief.

Agency: Commission for Human Rights
180 Westminster Street
Providence, RI 02903
401-222-7561
www.state.ri.us

SOUTH CAROLINA

Law: Code of Laws of South Carolina Sections 1-13-10 to
            1-13-100.

Scope: Employers, employment agencies, labor organiza-
            tions, but not employers with less than fifteen work-
            ers, public officials' staff, social membership clubs.
            (Secs. 1-13.30 and 1-13-80.)

Covers: It is an unlawful employment practice for an
            employer to fail or refuse to hire, bar, discharge from
            employment, or otherwise discriminate against an
            individual with respect to compensation, or terms,
            conditions, or privileges of employment because of
            sex, unless related to a bona fide occupational qual-
            ification which is reasonably necessary to the normal
            operations of the employer's business. (Sec.
            1302(A)(1), (I)(1).)

Remedies: Hiring, reinstatement, promotion, back pay (from
            which interim earnings are deducted), cease and
            desist orders, temporary restraining orders, attorney's
            fees, other appropriate relief.

Agency: South Carolina Human Affairs Commission
            P.O. Box 4490
            2611 Forest Drive
            Suite 200
            Columbia, SC 29204
            800-521-0725
            TDD 803-253-4125
            www.state.sc.us/schac

SOUTH DAKOTA

Law: South Dakota Codified Laws Annotated, Sections 20-13-1 to 20-13-56. South Dakota Human Relations Act.

Scope: Public and private employers, employment agencies, labor organizations. (Secs. 20-13-10 to 20-13-12.)

Covers: It is an unfair or discriminatory practice for any person, because of sex to fail or refuse to hire, to discharge or accord adverse or unequal treatment to any person or employee with respect to application, hiring, training, apprenticeship, tenure, promotion, upgrading, compensation, layoff or any term or condition of employment. (Sec. 20-13-10.)

Remedies: Hiring, reinstatement, promotion, back pay, cease and desist orders, other appropriate relief.

Agency: South Dakota Division of Human Rights
700 Governors Drive
Pierre, SD 57501
605-773-4493
www.state.sd.us/dcr/hr

TENNESSEE

Law: Tennessee Code Annotated, Sections 4-21-101 to 4-21-408. Tennessee Fair Employment Practices Law.

Scope: Public and private employers, employment agencies, labor organizations, but not employers with less than eight workers, domestic or certain family workers. (Secs. 4-21-102, 4-21-401.)

Covers: It is a discriminatory practice for an employer to fail or refuse to hire or discharge or otherwise to discriminate against an individual with respect to compensation, terms, conditions, or privileges of employment because of sex, unless based on a bona fide occupational qualification that is reasonably necessary to the normal operation of that particular business. (Secs. 4-21-401 and 4-21-406.)

Remedies: Hiring, reinstatement, promotion, back pay (from which interim earnings are deducted), cease and desist orders, temporary relief and restraining orders, money damages, attorney's fees, other appropriate relief.

Agency: Tennessee Human Rights Commission
530 Church Street
Suite 305
Cornerstone Square Building
Nashville, TN 37243-0745
615-741-5825
www.state.tn.us/humanrights

TEXAS

Law: Vernon's Texas Codes Annotated, Labor Code
Sections 21.001–21.051. Texas Commission on
Human Rights Act.

Scope: Public and private employers, employment agencies,
labor organizations, but not employers with less than
fifteen workers, certain family workers, political staff
or statewide hometown plan staff. (Secs.
21.051–.053, 21.002, 21.117, and 21.118.)

Covers: An employer commits an unlawful employment
practice if, because of sex, the employer fails or
refuses to hire an individual, discharges an individual or discriminates in any other manner against an
individual in connection with compensation, or the
terms, conditions, or privileges of employment,
unless related to a bona fide occupational qualification which is reasonably necessary to the normal
operations of the employer's business. (Sec. 21.051.)
Requires sexual harassment training for state
employees. (Sec. 21.010.)

Remedies: Hiring, reinstatement, promotion, back pay (from
which interim earnings are deducted), temporary
relief and restraining orders, attorney's fees to prevailing party, other appropriate relief.

continued

Agency: Commission on Human Rights
6330 Highway 290 East
Suite 250
P.O. Box 13006
Austin, TX 78711-3006
888-452-4778
TDD: 800-735-2989
www.state.tx.us

UTAH

Law: Utah Code Annotated, Sections 34A-5-101 to 108.
Utah Antidiscrimination Act.

Scope: Public and private employers, employment agencies,
labor organizations, but not employers with less than
fifteen workers, religious organizations. (Sec. 34A-5-
102.)

Covers: An employer may not refuse to hire, promote, discharge, demote, or terminate any person, or to retal-
iate against, harass, or discriminate in matters of
compensation or in terms, privileges, and conditions
of employment against any person otherwise qualified, because of sex unless based on a bona fide
occupational qualification. (Sec. 34A-5-106.)

Remedies: Reinstatement, back pay, benefits, cease and desist
orders, attorney's fees to prevailing plaintiff, other
appropriate relief.

Agency: Utah Antidiscrimination and Labor Division
160 East 300 South
Third Floor
Salt Lake City, UT 84111

Mailing:
P.O. Box 146630
Salt Lake City, UT 84114-6630
800-222-1238
TDD: 801-530-7685
www.ind-com.state.ut.us

VERMONT

Law: Vermont Statutes Annotated, Title 21, Sections 495, 495g. Vermont Fair Employment Practices Act.

Scope: Public and private employers, employment agencies, labor organizations, but not labor organizations that represent less than five workers. (Secs. 495 and 495d.)

Covers: It is an unlawful employment practice, except on the basis of a bona fide occupational qualification, for any employer to discriminate against any individual because of sex. (Sec. 495.) Sexual harassment is specifically covered as a form of sex discrimination and means unwelcome sexual advances, requests for sexual favors, and other verbal or physical conduct of a sexual nature when: (a) submission to that conduct is made either explicitly or implicitly a term or condition of employment; (b) submission to or rejection of such conduct by an individual is used as a component of the basis for employment decisions affecting that individual; or, (c) the conduct has the purpose or effect of substantially interfering with an individual's work performance or creating an intimidating, hostile or offensive work environment. (Sec. 495d.)

Remedies: Reinstatement, restitution of wages or benefits, injunction, damages, attorney's fees, other appropriate relief.

Agency: Vermont Attorney General
             Civil Rights Division
             109 State Street
             Montpelier, VT 05609-1001
             802-828-3171
             TTY: 802-828-5341
             www.atg.state.vt.us

VIRGINIA

Law: Annotated Code of Virginia, Sections 2.2-3900 to 2.2-3902. Virginia Human Rights Act.

Scope: Employers with at least five employees; State, its contractors and subcontractors with contracts of at least $10,000. (Secs. 15.2-1604 and 2.2-4200–4311.)

Covers: An unlawful discriminatory practice is conduct that violates any Virginia or federal statute or regulation governing discrimination on the basis of sex. (Sec. 2.2-3901.)

Remedies: Not specified, but back pay and other appropriate affirmative relief can be awarded.

Agency: Council on Human Rights
900 East Main Street
Pocahontas Building
Fourth Floor
Richmond, VA 23219
804-225-2292
www.chr.state.va.us

WASHINGTON

Law: West's Revised Code of Washington Annotated. Sections 49.60.010 to 49.60.320. Washington Law Against Discrimination.

Scope: Public and private employers, employment agencies, labor organizations, but not employers with less than eight workers, domestic and certain family workers, religious or nonprofit organizations. (Secs. 49.60.040 and 49.60.180–.200.)

Covers: The right to be free from discrimination because of sex is recognized as and declared to be a civil right. The right includes the right to obtain and hold employment without discrimination. (Sec. 49.60.030.) It is an unfair practice for any employer to refuse to hire any person because of sex, unless based upon a bona fide occupational qualification, or to discharge or bar any person from employment because of sex or to discriminate against any person in compensation or in other terms or conditions of employment because of sex. (Sec. 49.60.180.)

Remedies: Hiring, reinstatement, promotion, back pay, cease and desist orders, temporary relief or restraining orders, attorney's fees to prevailing plaintiffs (or defendants if case brought in bad faith), other appropriate relief.

Agency: Human Rights Commission
Olympia Headquarters Office
711 South Capitol Way
Suite 402
P.O. Box 42490
Olympia, WA 98504-2490
800-233-3247
TTY: 800-300-7525
www.hum.wa.gov

WEST VIRGINIA

Law: West Virginia Code, Sections 5-11-1 to 5-11-19. West
           Virginia Human Rights Act.

Scope: Public and private employers, employment agencies,
           labor organizations, but not employers with less than
           twelve workers, domestic and certain family work-
           ers, private clubs. (Sec. 5-11-3.)

Covers: Equal opportunity in employment is hereby declared
           to be a human right or civil right of all persons with-
           out regard to sex. (Sec. 5-11-2.) It shall be an unlaw-
           ful discriminatory practice, unless based upon a
           bona fide occupational qualification, or except
           where based upon applicable security regulations
           established by the United States or the state of West
           Virginia or its agencies or political subdivisions, for
           any employer to discriminate against an individual
           with respect to compensation, hire, tenure, terms,
           conditions, or privileges of employment if the indi-
           vidual is able and competent to perform the services
           required. (Sec. 5-11-9.)

Remedies: Hiring, reinstatement, promotion, back pay, cease
           and desist orders, attorney's fees to prevailing plain-
           tiff if case goes to court, other appropriate relief.

Agency: West Virginia Human Rights Commission
           1321 Plaza East
           Room 108A
           Charleston, WV 25301-1400
           888-676-5546
           www.wvf.state.wv.us/wvhrc

WISCONSIN

Law: West's Wisconsin Statutes Annotated, Sections 111.36(1)(b).

Scope: Public and private employers, employment agencies, labor organizations, but not certain family employers. (Secs. 111.32 and 111.325.)

Covers: It is an act of employment discrimination to refuse to hire, employ, admit or license any individual, to bar or terminate from employment or labor organization membership any individual, or to discriminate against any individual in promotion, compensation or in terms, conditions, or privileges of employment or labor organization membership because of sex. (Secs. 111.322 and 111.321.) Unless based on a bona fide occupational qualification, sex discrimination includes engaging in sexual harassment, or implicitly or explicitly making or permitting acquiescence in or submission to sexual harassment a term or condition of employment; or making or permitting acquiescence in, submission to or rejection of sexual harassment the basis or any part of the basis for any employment decision affecting an employee, other than an employment decision that is disciplinary action against an employee for engaging in sexual harassment in violation of this paragraph; or, permitting sexual harassment to have the purpose or effect of substantially interfering with an employees work performance or of creating an intimidating, hostile or offensive work environment. Sexual harassment also consists of unwelcome verbal or physical conduct directed at another individual because of that indi-

continued

viduals gender and that has the purpose or effect of creating an intimidating, hostile, or offensive work environment or has the purpose or effect of substantially interfering with that individuals work performance. Substantial interference with an employees work performance or creation of an intimidating, hostile, or offensive work environment is established when the conduct is such that a reasonable person under the same circumstances as the employee would consider the conduct sufficiently severe or pervasive to interfere substantially with the persons work performance or to create an intimidating, hostile, or offensive work environment. (Sec. 1136.)

Remedies: Appropriate relief, back pay (from which interim earnings are deducted).

Agency: Wisconsin Equal Rights Division
1 South Pinckney Street
#320
P.O. Box 8928
Madison, WI 53708
608-266-6860
TDD: 608-264-8752
www.dwd.state.wi.us/er

WYOMING

Law: Wyoming Statutes Annotated Sections 27-9-101 to 27-9-108. Wyoming Fair Employment Practices Act.

Scope: Public and private employers, employment agencies, labor organizations, but not employers with less than two workers, religious organizations. (Sec. 27-9-102.)

Covers: It is a discriminatory or unfair employment practice for an employer to refuse to hire, to discharge, to promote or demote, or to discriminate in matters of compensation or the terms, conditions, or privileges of employment against, a qualified disabled person or any person otherwise qualified, because of sex. (Sec. 27-9-105.)

Remedies: Hiring, reinstatement, promotion, back pay, cease and desist orders, other appropriate relief.

Agency: Wyoming Department of Employment
Labor Standards Division
Cheyenne Office
1510 East Pershing Boulevard
Suite 2015
Cheyenne, WY 82002
307-777-7261
http://wyoming.gov

appendix d:
References

AAUW, Hostile Hallways study.

C. Safran, "What Men Do To Women On the Job," Redbook Magazine (Nov. 1976) (reader questionnaire).

Cathy Redfern, "Female Cops Win Settlement, Lose Their Careers," Santa Cruz Sentinel (June 15, 2004).

Gail Gibson, "Similarities of Claims in Sex-Discrimination Lawsuits Against Morgan Stanely and Wal-Mart," Baltimore Sun, Journal Gazette (July 19, 2004).

"Hooters Suits Allege Climate of Harassment—Management of the Chain Say the Women Who Serve as Waitresses Are Put on a Pedestal," Orlando Sentinel, (July 20, 1993) at C6.

"'Hooters' Accord Reached," NAT'L L.J. (May 30, 1994) at A8 (quoting news release that states "the terms and conditions of the settlement [of all six Minneapolis suits] are confidential and all parties are satisfied with the resolution").

Jennifer Gould Keil, "Verdict in Sex Discrimination Lawsuit against UBS will likely Reverberate Throughout Financial Community." New York Post (April 10, 2005).

Lafontaine, E. and L. Treadeau, "The Frequency, Sources, and Correlates of Sexual Harassment among Women in Traditional Male Occupations," Sex Roles, pages 433–442 (1986) (160 women surveyed).

"LAPD Settles ACLU Sexual Assault Case for $165,000; Case Symbolizes Persistent Sexual Harassment, Gender Inequities" (Jan. 25, 1995).

Natasha Lorecki, "Ex-'Hooters Girl' wins $275,000 in Harassment Suit," Chicago Sun-Times (Nov. 24, 2004).

National Center for Women & Policing, "Equality Denied: The Status of Women in Policing," 2001 (April, 2002).

R. Sandroff, "Sexual Harassment: The Inside Story," Working Woman, p.47 (June 1992)).

"Sexual Harassment in the Coal Industry: A Survey of Women Miners. Oak Ridge, Tennessee: Coal Employment Project," as reported in New York Times (Oct. 22, 1991).

"Sexual Harassment: It's About Power, Not Lust," New York Times (Oct. 22, 1991).

"Two Out of Three Women in Military Study Report Sexual Harassment Incidents," The New York Times, p.A22 (Sept. 12, 1991).

U.S. Merit Systems Protection Board, Sexual Harassment of Federal Workers: Is it a Problem? Washington, D.C.: U.S. Gov't Printing Office (1981) (42%); U.S. Merit Systems Protection Board, Sexual Harassment of Federal Workers: An Update. Washington, D.C.: U.S.Gov't Printing Office (1987) (42%); and, U.S. Merit Systems Protection Board, Sexual Harassment in the Federal Workplace: Trends, Progress, Continuing Challenges. Washington, D.C.: U.S. Gov't Printing Office (1994) (44%).

Index

About the Author

Mary L. Boland received her law degree from John Marshall Law School in 1983. Since that time, she has worked as a legal advocate for victim's rights. She has authored legislation protecting victim's rights and has served as a consultant on projects for various public agencies. She is currently the co-chair of the Victim's Committee of the Criminal Justice Section of the American Bar Association and co-chair of the Victims Issues Committee of the Prosecutor's Bar Association of Illinois. She has also sat on many boards, task forces, and committees to develop better responses to sexual assault and sexual harassment victims in criminal and civil legal systems, including the Illinois Task Force on Gender Bias in the Illinois Courts, and the City of Chicago Advisory Council on Women, Violence Against Women Committee, which assisted in the preparation of sexual harassment policies and procedures for the City of Chicago.

The following highlight some of the books and articles Ms. Boland has authored.

- *Model Code Revisited: Taking Aim at the High-Tech Stalker*, American Bar Association, Criminal Justice Magazine (Spring 2005)
- *Collecting Child Support* (author, Sourcebooks 2004)

- *Your Right to Child Custody, Visitation and Support* (author, Sourcebooks Pub., 3rd Ed. 2004)
- *Sexual Harassment: Your Guide to Legal Action* (author, Sourcebooks 2002)
- *Enhancing Prosecution Through Victim-Sensitive Interviewing, Treatment and Preparation,* (chapter co-author) included in American Prosecutor's Research Institute, Prosecutor's Deskbook (2001)
- *A Crime Victim's Guide to Justice* (author, Sourcebooks 2nd Ed. 2001)
- *Domestic Violence: A Prosecutor's Guide* (author, Cook County State's Attorney's Office, 1996)
- *Sexual Assault: Issues and Recommendations* (expert contributor to ANew Directions, @ Crime Victims Agenda Project, U.S. Dept. of Justice, Office for Victims of Crime, 1996)

Ms. Boland is a full-time prosecutor and has been an adjunct professor at Governor's State University, Roosevelt University, and Loyola Law School in Chicago, Illinois.